Changing The Reflection

The Faces We Wear and the Truths They Hide

Alexis Carpenter

Copyright © 2024 by Alexis Carpenter

All rights reserved.

No part of this book may be reproduced in any form or by any electronic or mechanical means, including information storage and retrieval systems, without written permission from the author, except for the use of brief quotations in a book review.

This is a work of memoir. Some names, identifying details, and event sequences have been changed to protect the privacy of individuals involved. This memoir contains descriptions of real-life events that some readers may find distressing. Reader discretion is advised.

Cover: Dee Dee Book Covers
Author Photo Credit: Girl Squad Media

Paperback: 978-1-950476-97-8
Hardcover: 978-1-950476-98-5
Ebook: 978-1-950476-99-2

Dedicated to my sweet Jordan and big brother Shawn.

Foreword

By Jen Gottlieb

Isn't it amazing how sometimes the universe conspires to connect us with souls that resonate with ours, even through the most modern of mediums? My first encounter with Alexis wasn't your conventional IRL meet-and-greet; it unfolded in the comments and DM's first. Yep, I met Lexie on IG and I'm so grateful that the good ol' algorithm knew we needed to know each other.

Alexis is one of those people whose spirit transcends the screen; it's not just her words but the energy behind them. She was someone I felt I knew already, and of course we became fast "online friends." This online friendship developed into a real one when she started attending Build Your Brand Live events and masterminds. The moment we met off-screen was everything I expected it to be and more. She's the real deal.

"Changing The Reflection" is Alexis's inspiring journey captured on paper. It's more than a memoir; it's like sitting down with a friend who's been through the trenches but still sees the beauty in life. Alexis shares her experiences openly, covering both the tough times and the moments of light, making it incredibly relatable.

This book encourages us to take control of our narratives, especially if we've ever felt confined by others' perceptions. "Changing The Reflection" offers a guiding light for self-discovery and personal empowerment.

If you're looking for a read that's both inspiring and grounding, this book is exactly what you need. It's a reminder of the power of sharing our stories. Joining Alexis on her journey could be a step towards rediscovering your own strength and potential.

Letter to the Reader

For so many years, I thought about writing a book, especially about my life—since it's certainly been eventful—but like so many others, I was too scared to start. I was overwhelmed by the thought of being seen and judged. Have you ever felt like that? Like if the world saw you for who you truly are, you may be criticized or persecuted for just simply being yourself. This was a theme for me: having a burning desire, wanting something so much, and letting fear get in the way.

For a long time, I was going through life on autopilot, living but not actually living. This is the story of how I changed that.

This memoir is more than just my story; it's a promise to you. Maybe you feel like your dreams are unattainable fantasies because your appearance, dialect, or mannerisms don't mirror the conventional path to success. Or your soul has been battle-worn by the persistent whisper, "You are not enough," ringing in your ear and the trials you've encountered. This is your reminder that YOU are, in every sense, enough.

This book is for you, the go-getter, the resilient one, and the one who's always in motion. I see you, even when you feel like you're in a room and no one could possibly understand you. Perhaps you isolate yourself until you're forced to be around people. Maybe you even feel like you've had such shit luck that if you're around people, it'll rub off on them. It's not often anyone checks on you because you always seem to have it together, but inside you're crumbling. This book is your hope. Don't get me wrong, this book is very much a story of really fucking hard trials and tribulations, but even greater blessings in so many ways. It truly is all about perspective.

Life isn't a fairytale, and I won't spin it for you here, but I will tell you my truths. I will tell you that when I couldn't hold on anymore, God showed me the light. He would repeat, "Don't be afraid; I will protect you." I just had to remember (and still do) that without the darkness, we cannot understand the joy and privilege of having light.

On October 3, 2022, life as I knew it changed forever. That was the day our son, my beautiful bonus babe, Jordan Daniel Carpenter, was tragically taken from our family. At only twenty years old, so many dreams, hopes, and realities never got to see the light of day.

Two weeks later, I felt this overwhelming desire to write my story. It was like a desperation to share who I am, who he was, who my family is, and so much more. It was a bittersweet truth that the absence of love reminds you to be present. So, if you take anything from this book, let it be this: we all hear the stories and think, "It'll never happen to me," *until it does*. I was reminded in that moment how precious life is, how beautiful love is, and how impermanent we all are. Jordan gave me time, a voice, and the drive to share it.

When I die, I want the world to know my real story. My narrative will be told by me—not the one people create in their minds, not the rumors that are spread. Even worse, I don't want my stories to go untold because I was too scared to share them.

As I neared the completion of my memoir, another catastrophic life event brought me to my knees: my brother Shawn was gone. Cold and alone, he passed away just eight short months after our sweet Jordan. I blamed myself for his passing, even though I knew it wasn't my fault. But what if my sharing of this story sooner could have changed things? I've battled so many what-if's, but that's no way to live.

This book spills the secrets of my life, from a dark past to a future flickering with gentle light. My wish is that this is the push you need to stop waiting, to have hope, and to know you are perfectly imperfect with all of your scars, flaws, and past versions of yourself.

After you turn the last page, my hope is that a fire of confidence, hunger for change, and self-love builds within you. Your unique beauty is not just enough; it's a potent, invaluable blend of experiences, resilience, and hope.

Our circumstances, no matter how shameful they may feel, do not chain us to a fixed destiny. We hold the pen that writes our narrative.

So, my dear friend, I hope you are ready to venture off on this expedition with me, because it starts now.

While crafting this memoir, certain adjustments have been made to names, dates, and timelines. These changes serve a dual purpose: they enhance the depth and relatability of my stories while also safeguarding the privacy and dignity of the individuals. These modifications have been carefully balanced to preserve the essence and authenticity of each event, ensuring that the core spirit and truth of the stories remain intact.

Chapter 1

Letter To God

Dear God,

 Have you ever felt forgotten? Sure, everything that you do is seen (because it's expected), but "you" as a person (or God, in your case) are just blending into the background. I think being a strong person sometimes makes others forget that you're human (or, again, God, in your case), and that can hurt. Do you hurt like we do, God? I can imagine people are cruel to you (I know I've been; sorry about that). Or maybe people sometimes want to take more than they give, hide more than they show up, or only praise you when they feel you're "showing up" for them, then display cruelty when you don't meet their expectations.

I hope you don't mind, but sometimes I make up a new world (in my mind, of course) where I'm seen for who I am and all the insignificant things don't exist. Pleasing people isn't my top skill in this world because people want you to show up as YOU. My world is filled with beautiful smells, vibrant colors, people cherishing other people, and deeply feeling connection rather than greed or selfishness. I don't know.

I realize I just said I wanted to create a world better than yours… Let's hope I don't get smote by the almighty smiter (you). I mean this in the truest way, that respects everything you've created in our beautiful world. Shit—I mean, shoot—oh God, I'm sorry.

Just don't lose faith in me, God. I can do the things you've put me here to experience, even when they are hard, ugly, and painful. I know they can also be beautiful, loving, and filled with grace. I love you, G, and even though I don't go to church every Sunday anymore, I hold you in my heart and try to follow your guidance. We both know I'm not always good at it, but you still seem to show up for me time and time again. I believe this is why they call it "hope." You fill my soul with hope, and I blindly follow you every day.

 I love you, Lord, and am so thankful for this gift you've given me. The fact that you trust me with something so big that I can't even see its fullness yet tells me everything I need to know.

 Signing off—over and out.
 Your girl, Alexis

 Hmmm. Okay, wait, I'm back. I've just gotta ask: Will I ever be able to find my place in the world? Or is that place something I should stop looking for and make that space for myself? If we could have an expedited delivery on this answer, I'd appreciate it. No offense, God, but sometimes you be sending things through snail mail, and my anxious little self can't always handle that.

 P.S. Preferably, could this be a place that isn't defined by anyone else, but maybe you and me? Maybe, you know, we could sprinkle some of what I want in there, too. If not, I get it; your ideas are pretty cool, too. I mean, of course they are; you're GOD! Okay, I'm gonna let you get back to someone else's prayers.

 Goodnight—I mean, amen.

 Well, maybe one more thing, or ten. Who

knows? I'm still feeling some things, so I'll just leave them here, and we can follow up later.

Why is it that when we're tiny little kids, we don't seem to care if others think something is silly or too extreme? Now, as adults and even teens (at least for me), I'm this human with big emotions who feels everything so deeply. I'm also pretending nothing bothers me, laughing all the time and keeping a good attitude, but internally struggling, screaming on the inside because I refuse to release them out loud. Sometimes I think, What if one day, unexpectedly, I just wasn't here anymore? What would happen? What would people miss most?

I feel like my tasks and services would be missed the most, like meals, clothes, or maybe even a hug. But will they remember my gifts? You made me strong, creative, and passionate about life and people, but I don't think most see that. You gave me strength in vulnerability, and faith to put myself in positions where all the odds are stacked against me. I don't know if I'll ever get that answer, but I want to believe those things will begin to outshine the less meaningful things I do.

I want to be remembered for my heart, not my to-do list. How do we get people back to the reality of what's important and what's not? I know that's a loaded question since it's different for everyone, but it's not my fault you made an analyzer out of me.

It feels like I'm expected to have my shit together. ALL. THE. TIME. Never complain, stay small, be seen, and never be heard. But God, you gave me this big voice that keeps getting drowned out—surrounded by such noise that my own voice feels barely audible. I'm constantly haunted by the thoughts, What would happen if the world actually heard me? How would people react? How would people feel? If I no longer were that people-pleasing person, would they just drop me and find someone else who appeases them?

When I think about getting past my people pleasing, it's like the devil is laughing in my face, saying, "Okay, if you're no longer pleasing others, let's watch your worth disappear, and everyone you love to follow along with it." Sometimes, I feel abandoned by the world because I'm only worthy when I'm giving my full self to everyone else. There is no time for me, and when there is, it's selfish to take it. Lord, I will ask your permission first, but I'd really like to kick that devil right in the a—! Who does he think he is?

Okay, I got it! I'm not sure if anyone has ever thought of this genius plan, but here's my solution: When I start to see or think thoughts that only the devil himself could conjure, I'll say the word "pineapple," and you come down and karate chop him. It'll be a safe word that protects me from the devil. I'm sure there is another super-awesome, more faithful, classy word, but you know that ain't me! Luckily, you still love me anyway, because I'd be truly screwed if you didn't. Okay, pineapple is the word; please keep your all-hearing ears out for that daily whisper... "pineapple," hmmm. Okay, I'm not sure you fully understand the way this safe word works, but I'm gonna trust you. I'm sure you're the best karate chopper in the world, so I'll just let you be God!

Signing off, over and out!

P.S.S. Dang, sorry, one more thing: when I fully find my voice, I hope it's everything you planned for it to be. Thank you, Lord, for loving me unconditionally when no one else truly can. I love you, G.

Sincerely,
Alexis
I mean, amen.

Chapter 2

Living In A Nightmare

"Go back to that time when you were a little girl, boundless and free to express yourself just as you were," my mentor Jen directed, smiling brightly. I imagined she was reminiscing about that very version of herself.

The certainty in her words nudged me to try. I closed my eyes and dove straight into the depths of my soul to find little Alexis. In shock, my body started to react as if I'd just jumped from warm sand to subzero-temperature water. Heart racing, I saw red, and the undercurrent of panic set in as I frantically searched for that version of myself. The violent thrashes through the water were a suffocating reminder that the boundless and free version of me, *well, didn't exist.*

Let's hit the rewind button, and I'll take you through a blast from the past. It all started in a small apartment in the heart of Troy, New York, on November 19, 1987, around 9:30 p.m. My mom and dad got into a heated argument that quickly escalated into a physical altercation. The activity resulted in Mom's water breaking, leaving no time to think about what was happening. I'll spare you the details and fast-forward to the hospital room just five and a half hours later, where my mom screamed in agony in labor. Approximately twenty-four minutes later, at 3:24 in the wee hours of the mornin' on November 20, 1987, a not-so-loudly crying baby arrived. Yup, you guessed it, yours truly was born!

What would have been a touching moment was quickly overshadowed by the urgency of that damn umbilical cord wrapped around my neck. Talk about a bad day. I was supposed to be warm and cozy in my mom's belly for another month and five days, baking like a Christmas cookie, ready to be delivered on Christmas morning like Santa's presents. But nope, the argument, and apparently the universe, conspired and decided they'd give me a fight. You know, like survival of the fittest. Only I didn't have to try out for the show; I was volunteered as tribute.

Regardless, I clearly won the battle. The doctors heroically unwrapped the umbilical cord and examined my premature body. It was my not-so-developed lungs, trembling body, and other symptoms they were more concerned about at that moment. Amongst each other, in hushed whispers, they noted my symptoms resembled withdrawal from drug abuse, specifically crack cocaine.

Let's fast-forward to my first memories, when I was two years old and my mom was losing her battle with addiction. I'm sure she wanted to stop, but when you're stuck in a tainted environment, it's hard to dig yourself out. When hardship and dysfunction are everything you know and love, leaving can be the last solution you see until you're forced to. At least that's what happened to Mom. She was forced to get out, and my brother and I were caught in the line of fire as her life shifted forever.

This is when my brother and I were put in a foster home that, on the surface, was like any other. But beneath that façade, we experienced the kind of torment that was far from the love and protection a child is meant to feel. The house was old and gave *Haunted Mansion* vibes. You know, the one that has paint peeling and windows so clouded you'd think it had been abandoned for years. Yeah, *that* kind. But more than the home's aging appearance, there was a weight that clung to its walls, an atmosphere of gloom and unease. But Shawn and I were little, and it was the only world we really knew.

It felt like we were placed in foster care only to be forgotten after a short time. The home we were entrusted to used food as a tool for cruelty. Instead of warm meals that nourished our growing bodies, we were served squash morning, noon, and night—if and when we were fed at all. While other kids looked forward to a playful breakfast, we sat in harsh anticipation, wondering if today we'd be allowed to eat. Imagine your body leaping with joy for the same food merely because you're thankful to eat at all. To think cruelties like this still happen to kids in foster homes across America breaks me. We must do better.

I remember one sunny afternoon when the smell of summer was in the air. I sat on the porch, absorbed in the innocence of playing with building blocks. Lost in the simple joy of imagining a place where my mom, my brother, and I lived where pain was a distant memory. A brief moment out of my reality, but that escape was shattered when a metal Tonka truck, with all its cold, unbending weight, struck my fragile little face. Thrown maliciously by the foster parents' son. My world was instantly shrouded in pain, stars, and tears as awareness sunk its claws deep into my tiny heart.

Before I could even register what just happened, Shawn was by my side, his anger a palpable force against the injustice I'd suffered. He cradled me, trying to soothe the soundless tears that streamed down my face. His grip was both a protective shield against the world and a reflection of his own fear of the repercussions that were bound to come. And they did.

They sent us to our separate rooms, trying to tear apart the only source of comfort we had. *Each other*. I was placed in a crib in the hallway, just outside their bedroom, as a reminder of their dominance. Shawn was confined to a room upstairs, locked away from me and everyone else.

We constantly faced dilemmas like this which spoke volumes about the twisted environment we lived in. There was no way out of his locked room, so this particular night, when he had to go to the bathroom, he had to resort to peeing in a cup. He naively hoped to spare himself from further punishment—our foster parents were always looking for an excuse to punish us. But this time, when they shouted profanities as they ascended the stairs, he felt a slight victory. He had already drunk the pee before they could find the cup, careful not to leave any traces of his defiance for a crime that should never have existed. The bile that threatened to expose him was the only evidence confirming his rebellion, and by the grace of God, he was able to hold it back.

With a diaper that grew heavier with each passing minute, I became the fix they were looking for. Dissatisfied with their findings in Shawn's room, they set their eyes on another target: me. So, when it was finally noticed that my diaper was soggy and drooping, punishment was inevitable. Each blow felt like a reinforcement of my worthlessness; the pure disgust in their eyes just happened to be my confirmation.

And yet, through it all, the silent promise between Shawn and me remained unbroken. A promise that, as long as we had each other, we would find the strength to keep going. We hoped and prayed for a better tomorrow. Our story is a symbol of the resilient spirit of siblings, who, in the face of unspeakable cruelty, found strength in each other.

In the heart of the darkness, there were pockets of hope—small flashes of light that created flickers of a flame for my tiny soul. One of those hopeful moments took place about a year later when we visited Mom at rehab. It was like drawing a breath of fresh air after being submerged under water for what felt like eternity.

The ride to see her was always filled with anxiety and anticipation. The sterile smell of the rehabilitation center would immediately hit me when we walked into that cold gray stone building. To me, it was a welcome contrast to the odd odor at our foster home that seemed to linger heavily. But none of that mattered the moment I'd see my mother's face. The rest of the world blurred; my heart, which was usually guarded and wary, would burst open, allowing her love to pour in.

This particular visit, I remember she had surprises for us. My fingers traced the contours of the brand-new Barbie, with real rubber bendable legs—a luxury compared to the hollow plastic, one-armed, and short-haired doll I was used to. I looked over at my brother's face and felt warmth inside when I saw him beaming with joy as he marveled at his G.I. Joe, lost in the world of action and adventure.

We got to have a small picnic in the backyard of the rehab that day. It felt as if time had stopped, allowing us a momentary escape from reality. We laughed, shared stories, and basked in the love of our mother. This is what life should have felt like all the time. Sun on our faces, laughing with the ones we loved, and filling our heart with joyful memories. I felt lighter than I had in months. It was a day etched into my memory so deeply that it's time-stamped as a demonstration of the healing power of love. Strangely, I don't remember ever visiting Mom after that day.

The harsh reality of our lives returned all too quickly, and the days morphed into a monotonous procession of shadows. Until we were granted another ray of hope. Shawn and I were picked up from the foster home and brought to our Nana and Papa's house in Vermont. Their house was a sanctuary, a haven filled with the aroma of freshly baked cookies, soft blankets, real beds, and comforting lullabies.

One of the last nights I remember being at Nana and Papa's, the yummy-smelling chicken and Nana's famous garlic mashed potatoes sat invitingly on the table. I remember how the warm, buttery texture would melt in my mouth; each spoonful felt like a warm hug. Nana kept reminding us to slow down so we didn't get tummy aches, but it's hard to trust the food in front of you when you've been shown how quickly it can be taken away. Shawn and I were in our own world; his infectious laughter echoed mine. Each time he'd whip his head around to make silly faces or funny noises, my giggles grew louder. I'm not sure how it was possible, but my view of him as a superhero grew even bigger. He was my sun, radiating love and protection, and I was the moon in a dark sky. We were all each other had, and that was our peace. It had to be.

After dinner, I watched Shawn morph into this adult-like figure. It was astonishing to me since he was only five years old. A small but mighty protector of his three-year-old little sister. He cleaned my face with so much care; his touch was ever so gentle as he wiped away the remaining food from dinner. This was a pretty big project since I'd manage to get food everywhere: clothes, hair, face, up my nose—it was a never-ending task. Holding onto my tiny but pudgy little fingers, he'd guide me upstairs, and get me ready for bed while singing our favorite songs. I'd always notice the slight tremble in his voice when he'd say, "I love you, Lexie. Goodnight." It was always filled with a sadness that seemed far too mature for a five-year-old.

We grew accustomed to the repetitive cycle of being whisked away to their warm embrace only to be yanked back to the foster home without warning. So we would enjoy the moments we had while we had them, never expecting anything more or anything less. Let me tell ya, that will change your perspective on appreciating the little things. Social and Rehabilitation Services, also known as SRS at the time, would appear like clockwork for an unwelcome visit. These visits were moments of pure terror. Their stern faces and sharp words made my stomach hurt just as fast as I could blink. They were insensitive and their words felt like blades hot enough to slice through reality like it was butter.

To no surprise, just as quickly as it came, the serenity of that evening, at Nana and Papa's eating chicken around the table together, was shattered the next morning, which began early with chaos. The familiar voices of my grandparents, usually soft and gentle, were filled with urgency and distress. I didn't know what was going on, and as my heart raced, only one thought crossed my mind: *Where's Shawny?*

My feet barely touched the ground as I raced downstairs to the kitchen table. Hiding beneath its concealing, long tablecloth seemed like the only safe place. But that safety evaporated when the sudden, painful grip on my ankle jolted me back to the horrifying reality. Tears blurred my vision, and I felt a raw desperation as I screamed for release, holding a table leg like my little life depended on it. And then I heard Shawn yell, his voice trembling with rage and fear, "Get your hands off my s-si-sister!" Our tears merged as he dove under the table and embraced me.

Later that day, we found ourselves in a courtroom. The world was a whirlwind of voices, faces, and decisions being made over our heads. Unbeknownst to us at the time, the judge's decree sealed our fate, severing our connection to Nana and Papa and declaring our destiny for the coming months. The finality of the gavel signaled the conclusion of our situation. We were devastated when we realized what was happening. I wish someone would have told us it wasn't because our grandparent's home wasn't the best place for us; it was a flaw due to our position, caught between two states' judicial systems.

The car ride back to the foster home was a blur of grief. The four and a half hours felt like an eternity, with every mile increasing the distance between us and the love we knew. The world outside zoomed past, but inside, time seemed to crawl, every second punctuated by the sting of tears and the ache of separation.

Shawny grasped my hand a little tighter in that moment, a silent pledge that no matter where they took us, we'd always have each other. The unspoken promise between us was a piece of hope I'd hold on to forever.

Chapter 3

Coming Home

My mom fought hard to get my brother and me back from the foster home after getting clean. She was so proud when we got to visit for the day, and she would have cans of raviolis or beefaroni stocked in the cupboard. The SRS worker would reward her with a "good job" or "keep up the great work!" I loved it because the more the lady said good job to my mom, the more I got to see her. The last time the case worker came was for a final evaluation of our living conditions when I was six. This visit would determine whether or not my brother and I could live with my mom again. I held my breath with every checkmark on her clipboard.

"Well, Penny, congratulations! You've done an outstanding job getting your home in order—it looks great. You have food for the kids and they have a bedroom they can call theirs. I'll come back in two weeks for a final check, but as of right now, you're being granted temporary custody of your children." The SRS worker smiled brightly at me and asked, "Do you know what that means, sweetheart? You get to stay with your mommy!"

I matched her bright smile with a toothy grin of my own. I squealed, ran to my mom, and hugged her tightly.

We spent the first night having a family game night.

Our Nana and Papa came over and celebrated with bubbling pizza, bags of chips, and those Big Slam Pepsi and Mountain Dew sodas. And of course we had the trifecta of games: Monopoly, Uno, and Skip-Bo were our favorites. This particular game night was the best. It was a moment that represented freedom, family, and fun. Game and pizza night became a sacred Friday night in our household; it was the one time a week that it seemed like the world stood still just for us—me, my mom, and my brother. We didn't need any fancy restaurant reservations or overpriced trips to an amusement park. Nah, our joy was homegrown, harvested right from the dining room table, surrounded by mismatched chairs.

We would play Monopoly, and let me tell ya, it was a marathon. Oh, how my brother and I loved the feeling of becoming pretend business moguls, buying up pretend properties with pretend money. Mom usually dominated the board, collecting those green houses like they were going out of style. But every so often, one of us would land on Free Parking and claim a pile of money, becoming a mini-Rockefeller for a few delirious minutes.

"Ah, you kids!" Mom would jokingly say, shaking her fist in the air.

Then there was Uno, the game that could turn on a dime. One minute I'd be laughing, and the next I'd be glaring at my brother for slapping down a Draw Four. It was the great equalizer. Even if you had been destroyed in Monopoly, redemption was just a "Reverse" card away. My brother had this sneaky way of hoarding Wild cards, and just when you thought you had him cornered—BAM!—he'd unleash his rainbow-colored arsenal. It was complete BS and cheating, if you ask me.

By this point, we'd usually be nursing the last sips of our Big Slams and Mountain Dews, the pizza box left only with crumbs and stray pieces of pepperoni. Overtired and giggling, our tiny little eyes would close against our will. At which point the clock told us it was far past our bedtimes. But none of us cared. We were together, bonded over cardboard, plastic, and the simplest joys of life.

We spent a ton of time making up for the five and a half years we spent apart and making memories to hold us over in case anything happened. Mom was especially aware that the SRS worker still needed to return and finalize the order for us to remain home permanently.

The two weeks passed and it was time for another inspection. This time, Mom was prepared. We had a house stocked with food, our rooms set up, and plenty of clothes and toys, all representing a well-maintained house. We were bathed and Mom had us on our best behavior, giving that side eye when we stepped out of line, a quick indicator to tighten up. *This is serious business.* Shawn and I would usually look at each other and giggle, of course ultimately behaving because we didn't want to mess up our chance to stay with our mom.

"She's here," my mom said a little nervously as she tugged on our clothes to smooth them out, did a little lick of her hand, and slicked Shawn's hair to the side. He gagged and said, "Ewww, Moooommmm!" I just chuckled and put on my cutest smile. The toothy, big-cheek smile that could light up a room.

The lady came in and started walking around like before, but this time she had someone else with her. This made me a little nervous, and I found myself tucking behind my brother. He grabbed my hand.

"It's okay, Lex," Shawny said in his bravest voice.

The tour was done and the results were in. I think we all held our breath and anticipated the lady's response.

"Well, you should be really proud of yourself, Penny." We all exhaled. "You have turned things around for you and your kids. We're excited to tell you that your custody has been granted. Congratulations and keep on this journey."

This is the moment our full-time life in Vermont began. This is how families are supposed to be—together.

Chapter 4

Skin Color Isn't Contagious

A YEAR into living with Mom, I started school. Feeling like a big girl at seven years old, I squealed with excitement all morning as my mom put me in a pair of pink floral leggings and a white top with the matching pattern on the collar. I was truly feeling fabulous, especially with my hair in pigtails that were gelled into spiral curls. There was a little resolve since this would be the first time I had to go anywhere without my brother. For kindergarten in Vermont, kids went in the afternoon, so I had a different bus. *Today is the day I will make so many new friends,* I thought to myself.

My mom and I walked to the bus stop and waited anxiously for my first bus ride on the first day of school, and I wondered who would be my very first friend. I looked around and quickly noticed I was a little different than everyone at the bus stop. Then it seemed like their parents were looking at me with disgust; some even held their kids back from talking to me. When we all got on the bus, it felt like a literal scene from *Forrest Gump* where all the kids slid to the end of the seat, looked up, and said, "This seat is taken." One kid told me to go to the front of the bus because I wasn't allowed to sit with the "normal people."

I didn't want to be on that bus anymore. I jumped when the driver snapped at me. "Let's go, kid. Find a seat and sit down now!" Tears pricked my eyes as I looked back toward the front, tripped over a kid's foot, and eventually made my way to a seat three rows from the front. A few tears fell, but I quickly wiped them away so no one would see.

I started thinking about my family—my mom, brother, and grandparents—and realized everyone else looked different than me, too. With their white skin, they seemed to blend in with everyone else around me, but my having a black father caused me to stand out like a dandelion in a field of roses. At that moment, I had an internal conflict stirring that I'd never felt before. I suddenly realized I lived in a town where no one looked like me, everyone was white, and I felt out of place.

Society only seemed to validate my fears each day. I was called weird and an outcast. I was told I had dirty skin and needed to take a bath. Kids would joke, "Get the hose and wash this dirty rat." I wanted to run far away each and every day of my life. *Why the hell did I have to look like this?* I began paying attention to everything and everyone and noticed I'd rarely even seen girls who looked like me on TV, in magazines, or in books.

I just wanted to be like everyone else, but I wasn't, and I couldn't control that fact. I did the walk of shame every day to the bus stop, feeling responsible for something outside my control—how I looked. At such a young age, I carried an earth-shattering desperation to die rather than feel the hateful gazes of kids who would never give me a chance. This shame felt permanent and unforgiving.

Most of the bullying happened on the bus or in the cafeteria at school. Kids pointing their fingers would cause me to hang my head in defeat while they stared and sneered in undeniable disgust. This always left a gnawing feeling throughout my body that I couldn't shake, from my feet, which housed the pink Power Ranger shoes two sizes too big we found at the AMES department store for six dollars, to my high-water jeans. I heard everything from "Look at the black clown coming with her welfare shoes" to "The nigger must be waiting for a flood with pants over its ankles like that," whispered by my classmates in the cafeteria.

We didn't have much money for new clothes, so my mom would get hand-me-downs from neighbors. Up until this point, I was excited to receive the new-to-me clothes. Sometimes, we'd find outfits for five dollars at J.J. Newberry's. I loved going to Newberry's when my Nana and Papa would come with us, especially when I could get a blueberry muffin and hot cocoa from the diner inside. It wasn't just any blueberry muffin; it was the *best* blueberry muffin in the world, with the big sugar speckles covering the top. And, if I were a good girl, Nana would let me get whipped cream on my hot cocoa! Gosh, I loved those memories and often found myself holding onto that feeling when I was surrounded by nothing but hate.

Always misunderstood, the outsider with chocolate skin and dark eyes, I'd head back to the sea of kids so different from me. I wondered what that day would bring—more names, getting hit, or just feeling oceans apart from anyone in the world who could possibly understand me. My heart beat the same as theirs, yet they treated me like the color of my skin was contagious, like if they came too close, they'd be infected by my misfortune.

Thinking about standing six feet apart now is so normal, but when you're a seven-year-old brown girl in an all-white elementary school in Newport, Vermont, where most don't even know you exist, it hurts. Judged solely on the external factors that identified me, features I couldn't change, I prepared myself for a life filled with hurt and misunderstanding.

I didn't know much about being black other than that it's the vessel I show up in every day. A color that changed what the world thought of me and how I was treated. Eventually, I had no choice but to blend into the background, change everything about myself, hope no one saw me, and pray the ones that did weren't cruel. Everyone I loved became my defense, my armor, and my camouflage.

I dreaded going to the cafeteria and facing my first-grade school bully, Amber. I don't know what I ever did to her, but she was determined to make every day of my life as miserable as possible. Her preferred vehicles of hatred included dumping food on me, pushing me off the bench, tripping me, taking my food, dumping milk on my food, and so many more cruel things. I felt most anxious in the cafeteria, vulnerable and exposed, waiting for someone to torment me or say brutal things I'd repeat to myself later that day when I got home. Being alone is what I'm good at. But one day I heard a small voice beside me, barely audible.

"Can I sit here with you?"

Mouth agape, I slowly turned my head to meet this person who obviously didn't know the rules. You'd think there was a sign posted: "Alexis sits alone at this terrible blue table, on an island away from everyone else." I looked around, wondering if I was being punk'd, and caught Amber sneering at me as if I willed this girl to come talk to me.

"You don't want to sit here?" I met her gaze and quickly looked down. "This isn't really the table kids sit at." My voice was filled with anxiety as flashes of Amber's rage played in my head.

Completely unphased, she responded, "Okay… can *I* sit with you?"

I nodded slowly, wondering if she was about to do something other than just sit down. Would she dump her chocolate milk on my head like Amber did the day before, or maybe dump food on me like Amber did earlier that week, or whatever other cruel thing she could have possibly been planning? Her eyes didn't seem to tell that story, though; she seemed (dare I say it?) *kind*. She took a seat across from me. After dipping her slice of pepperoni pizza in ranch, she took a big bite and, with a full mouth, said,

"I'm Charlene—well, I'm Esperanza, but no one can pronounce my name, so I go by my middle name, Charlene. What's your name?"

Just as I opened my mouth to tell her my name, she started talking again. I silently chuckled, wondering where in the world someone like her came from, and at that moment I realized I had no idea who she was. I'd never seen her before; she must have been a new student.

A lump formed in my throat, my heart ached, and my nose began to prickle when I realized this is what it felt like to have someone show you kindness. Charlene was a good person, unbothered by my differences, and for the short two minutes before the bell rang, indicating lunch was over, I felt peace, acceptance, and happiness. I wanted to hold on to those feelings. I didn't say a word. I just listened and allowed myself to take in the moment I'd craved for the whole seven years of my existence.

For the first time in my life, I felt genuinely seen by another human being. Ironically, it was also in the school cafeteria, where every clatter of trays and laughter had previously seemed to spotlight my isolation. Charlene shattered the walls of loneliness that I had built up over the years. I was always braced for the next insult, the next humiliation, preparing my spirit for the next blow. I was in a prison within my solitude, and then Charlene happened. I still believe she was sent to me from the angels above, because life with her in it had purpose, and she taught me so much about being a good person in just two short minutes. She didn't see the invisible "Keep Out" sign that I thought was posted above my head. She *saw* me.

When the bell rang, ending my momentary paradise, I felt a sting of sadness, but I also felt something I hadn't felt in what felt like years: a flicker of hope. It was a short lunch, but its impact was beyond measure. Charlene, with her pepperoni pizza and her effortlessly-given kindness, showed me that life could be different, maybe even fun. She gave me a taste of what it was like to not dread the simple things—the acts of existing in a shared space with someone I'd never met. I didn't know if I'd feel that way again anytime soon, but I knew that I wanted to hold onto that moment for as long as I could, like my life depended on it. I guess, in a way, it kind of did.

Later that night, I was sitting on my lawn at home and looked down the street to see a U-Haul; someone new was moving in. I saw four little girls and maybe a mom and dad. I must have let my thoughts wander because when I came back to reality, a pack of girls were halfway to me. Instinctively, I froze, then darted inside. *This would be the moment I got jumped and eaten alive by a group I didn't even know.* I shut and locked the door, but just a few seconds later, the gang of girls were on my porch. They were dressed differently than I'd ever seen before, with crazy, wild hair and wearing bright smiles.

The knock on the door startled me, but the giggles and chatter made me curious. "I think it's Charlene," I said so softly that even I could barely hear it. I went to the door and opened it to see Charlene and three other girls returning my gaze with cheeky smiles. I don't think I said a word. I stood in shock.

"Hey, it's me, Charlene! Remember from school lunch today? Do you want to come out and play with me and my sisters Anna, Christina, and Val?"

My mouth fell open. No one ever wanted to play with me, and if they talked to me, it was usually to make fun of me, or do something cruel. They all looked at me expectantly. I slammed the door in their faces, ran upstairs, and yelled, "Mom, can I go outside and play with the new girls on our street?" I was already running back downstairs as she yelled, "Sure!"

I swung open the door, and they were gone. My smile fell and my shoulders slumped, until I heard one of the girls.

"I guess she doesn't want to play. Let's go home."

I pushed through the screen door, startling them this time.

"Sorry," I giggled sheepishly, "I had to ask my mom if it was okay to come out and play. I don't really have friends, so I don't ever play anywhere else. I don't even know what to play!"

"You can come see our house if you want!" Christina belted, and we all laughed and shook our heads in excitement.

I followed them to their house, marking the beginning of a lifetime of friendship. The start of understanding what it meant to have a friend—well, more like a pack. I finally knew what it felt like to be accepted by people outside my own family. That became an addiction, something I would seek forever.

As we walked toward Charlene's house, I observed the way they carried on in conversation with each other and realized I had started to mimic their movement and body language. God, I was so awkward, but so brave, if I do say so myself. I didn't have role models to demonstrate how to show up and present myself, so I learned by watching and mirroring others. Seeing the world through Charlene's eyes was like living in a whole new world—a beautiful one filled with color, love, and freedom.

I'd been told that I didn't belong my whole life—in the cafeteria, at the bus stop, in my foster home, and eventually I'd even feel that way at my dining room table and so many other places. Maybe I was just beginning to discover the people and places I did belong around. As I walked with Charlene, Anna, Christina, and Val towards their house, I felt like I was walking into a new life. For the first time, the feeling of emptiness began to fill with something I had long thought was a fairytale: *belonging*.

I was a master observer that day. Watching their interactions and how natural their movements were; the ease with which they laughed and talked. I literally felt like a student of life, absorbing lessons I'd never been taught at home or in school: how to be a friend, how to accept kindness, and how to laugh without waiting for the other shoe to drop. Charlene and her sisters unknowingly taught me that day. It was a gift that no school could ever offer.

I had spent so much time in fear, apprehensive of new faces, expecting the worst because history taught me to. I just couldn't believe how one person's heart shattered all of that by sitting next to me. She and her family demolished my thick walls that day, becoming my safe place.

Charlene's house was like stepping into another universe—a place where love wasn't rationed and kindness wasn't conditional. We played games and laughed until our bellies hurt, and for a few hours, I just got to be a kid. No demands from my home life; no fear of bullies; just a normal kid. That night, when the streetlamps came on, I went back home, but I was lighter, almost as if the weight of my extended isolation had been lifted.

Being welcomed into Charlene's home wasn't just about fun and games; it was an initiation into what life could be. And I was hooked. I wanted more days like that, more moments that felt like a part of something bigger. And not just to be part of a group, but to find pieces of the little girl I stared back at every day in the mirror that I didn't even know were missing.

That night in bed, I thought about that stroll down the street. It was like the beginning of my journey to a new world all together. A journey that started with mimicking but eventually led to finding my voice, my laughter, and my way of being in their presence—and eventually maybe even the world. That night, after a full day of play and feeling accepted, I closed my eyes, a smile on my face, and whispered, "Maybe I do belong; maybe we all have a place we fit in, a table we're welcomed at, a world where we're seen." The lesson Charlene taught me that day was one that I'd carry with me for the rest of my life. A lesson that gave me a glimpse of kindness and hope that things I had never imagined were possible for someone like me.

Chapter 5

The Vacuum Chase

Despite having no friends up until I met Charlene and her sisters, growing up, I could always count on my brother Shawn. We were two peas in a pod, thick as thieves, partners in crime; you name it. Our shared antics were the stuff of family legends —some tear-jerking, some stomach-aching laughter—but all unforgettable. One story in particular stands out above the rest and gets retold every year, much to the amusement (and slight embarrassment) of my mom.

It started like any other day of third grade in late August 1996. I was returning home from school, and as usual, I found my brother Shawn caught up in some squabble with a neighborhood kid at the bus stop. He was the only ten-year-old I knew who fought that much. Something didn't sit well when I realized the person he was fighting with was a jerk named Josh.

I may not have had the courage to defend myself, but when it came to Shawn, I was a fiercely protective eight-year-old little sister, and I certainly wasn't about to stand by. So, in a fit of rage (and probably a sprinkle of stupidity), I gave Josh a hard shove (which barely made him move). In return, I received a sharp kick to my stomach from his steel toe boots.

"Ouch!" I moaned.

Crying and clutching my stomach, my brother rushed me home. We found Mom immersed in her weekly house-dusting ritual. Between my sobs, I tried to explain to her what happened, but because of her frantic concern (and possibly the noisy vacuum), she misunderstood and assumed that the culprit was my brother.

Without warning, she detached the vacuum hose and started chasing him. I watched, wide-eyed, as she pursued Shawn around the house, hose in hand, yelling, "Why would you kick your sister in the stomach?!"

Shawn ran in circles, laughing. "Mom!" he yelled. "It wasn't me!" All the while, I trailed behind them both, gasping through tears of pain and laughter, trying to declare Shawn's innocence.

"Shawn! Get over here!" my mother's voice boomed from the kitchen. The vacuum's loud humming made for pretty comical background music as she lunged at my brother, the vacuum hose raised again like some kind of medieval weapon. Shawn's eyes, wide as saucers now, dodged just in time, shooting me an "is she for real?" glance.

I stood there, still clutching my aching stomach, tears streaming down my face, but not entirely from pain. It was hard not to laugh at the ridiculousness of the scene in front of me. Shawn, our family's resident troublemaker, darted from one room to another, trying to put as much furniture between him and the menacing vacuum hose. "Mom! Really, it wasn't me!" he hollered again while skidding around the dining table.

My efforts to chime in with the actual story were constantly interrupted by fits of giggles. "Mom, he didn't... he didn't... oh my gosh, look out for the vase!" I finally managed to sputter out between bursts of laughter.

By the time the merry chase concluded, our living room looked like a war zone. Tumbled chairs, a flipped cushion, and the three of us collapsed in a heap, gasping for air; a combination of the run and fits of laughter.

"Okay, okay," I finally got out, sitting up and wiping tears from my cheeks. "*Josh* kicked me, not Shawn! I pushed Josh because he was picking on Shawn, and he got back at me by kicking me with his stupid steel toe boots."

The realization of her comical mistake washed over Mom's face. "Oh, shit! Sorry, bud, I thought she said, Shawn." She turned her apologetic gaze to him, who just smirked back at me.

"Maybe lead with that next time, Lex?" Shawn suggested.

With the vacuum hose now lying defeated on the couch, I continued to convey the day's events to our still-exasperated mom. Shawn was cleared of all charges, and the great vacuum chase became an integral chapter in our bank of family stories.

Gosh, I'm so grateful for memories like this one. Even through adversity—bullying, torment, and hurt—there were countless moments of uncontrollable laughter. So, if you asked me how I coped with challenging times, it was times like these. I didn't have many friends, but I had something even better—a best friend in my brother. The power of our love, laughter, and joy built a resilience in me that I hadn't realized.

I hope you get to experience joy like this—the kind of joy that becomes a favorite story at the dinner table or is retold every year during the holidays. These are the moments that propel us forward. So, I say more of *this*, please.

Chapter 6

Quiet Keeps You Safe

I was talking with my mentor Amber recently, and it triggered a core memory when she asked about safety. "Does it feel safe when you use your voice? Did it ever not feel safe for you to use your voice? Is there something or someone you feel safe using your voice with?" Staring at her blankly, I was conflicted inside, but there was this deep-rooted pain I couldn't put my finger on.

"Take a moment and sit with it for a bit," she continued. "And tell me, what does that mean for you? What is safety?" A string that had hemmed my emotions in was pulled with that question, and the floodgates broke open. I was instantly overwhelmed with emotion, realizing for the first time that I didn't even know what safety meant because I spent my life in survival mode and hadn't experienced it.

Somewhere along the way, I learned that being myself, and saying anything other than what someone told me to say, was dangerous. Punishments would come, people would abandon me, and uncertainty would settle in. Performing became a way for me to navigate things in a way that felt secure but not quite safe. My performances got bolder as I got older, and it's only now that I can see the path of disaster I set myself on. I now have an idea of what safety means, but the years I spent without it have left an indelible mark.

When I was eight, my mom had double knee surgery. She suffered from arthritis and Lupus, so fluid and deteriorating bones were constantly causing her pain. Since she was bedridden for several weeks, my stepdad took me to my hair appointment. I loved having fun moments with Dad, and I hoped this would be one of them. He was there for me over the last couple of years when Mom and he got together. As long as I was a good girl and listened to what mom said we needed to do, everything would be fine. My mom gave my stepdad specific instructions to relay to the stylist at my appointment.

"You got all that, Pooper?" he asked when she finished. I cringed inside every time he used that stupid nickname. It was embarrassing and left me feeling frustrated.

"Yes, Dad. Mom said, 'A trim and nothing more. The most she should take off is two inches,'" I recited. I ran and got my jacket on since it was a measly thirty degrees outside.

We drove a few blocks to the salon, listening to Johnny Cash's "Ring of Fire," singing loudly. Before I knew it, we pulled up to Ladies and Lords Hair Salon. At least that's what it was called at the time, but its name and ownership changed at least three times throughout my childhood. I had this weird feeling in the pit of my stomach, but I chalked it up to being hungry since I missed my traditional breakfast of Kix with a pound of granulated sugar and milk.

I skipped my happy little self into the salon with my stepdad and went straight to the front counter. The receptionist's eyes grew wide, and I shrank a little. Taking my dad's hand, I scooted my petite eight-year-old body behind him so I was barely visible. He yanked me back beside him, blowing my cover.

"Come on, get out of there. The lady needs you." She just kept looking at me like I was not supposed to be there. Eventually, after what felt like a year, we walked toward a woman with short blonde hair, glasses, and a face full of dark makeup. It was a bit scary and intimidating.

I'll never forget the look because every salon lady in Newport seemed to get it in their eyes when looking at my hair, telling me they had no idea what the hell they were doing. That should have been my cue to get out of there faster than the pit crew changing a NASCAR tire—before someone had me looking like a freak.

My entire life, I've lived outside the norm. I have been automatically deemed a bad person by many because of the color of my skin. As a little kid, I didn't understand it, but I see it now. I understand why I molded myself into a shapeshifter who would do anything for anyone and be the girl everyone wanted me to be—to truly know me wasn't an option many chose. I didn't feel worthy of living authentically because the rules everyone lived by didn't apply to me. I was "different."

Most of my childhood I grew up cast as the poor black girl who showed up in pink Power Ranger shoes too big for her feet, wearing high-water jeans, and with a gap-toothed smile. My mom never knew how to care for my hair, so she would brush out my curls, causing my bangs (yes, you read that right... *bangs*) to frizz and sit like a dust ball that built up in an old house over a year's time on top of my chocolate forehead. I still have the school picture as my witness. It was awful.

She used to threaten that if I didn't like the way she did my hair, she would shave it all off. That was *the most terrifying* statement, especially as an eight-year-old brown girl in a school where everyone already hated me. Could you imagine the shit that would have caused? Man, that one gives me nightmares... *still*.

This only made going to the salon that much scarier.

"Just a trim, please." I told the lady after a pause. "My mom said no more than two inches."

"Okay," was all she replied.

As I watched her in the mirror touching my hair in disgust, I slouched, feeling gross in my own skin. She, too, brushed ALL my hair until my beautiful curls were gone. The hair that once fell to the middle of my back was now so big that you could barely see my face. When I was brave enough to lift my head again, my eyes went wide in horror. I knew this was going to end badly. With dry, now-puffed-out hair, she began cutting... and cutting. This time, it was her eyes that went wide. Her mouth parted as she took a sharp inhale, then she turned the chair so I was no longer looking in the mirror. She walked away to get another woman who began in on my hair—that was scarily feeling lighter and lighter on my head. She tipped my chair, washed it, blew it dry, and turned me to face the mirror. *That can't be me.* Looking back at me was a girl with a mushroom cut.

Tears welled up in my eyes as I met her gaze in the mirror.

"Sorry," she said, genuinely apologetic. "We don't know how to treat your people's hair." I was so ashamed and embarrassed, and I knew without a doubt that I would be in serious trouble when I got home. The actions of others were always a reflection of me; at least that's how it felt when I would get in trouble.

I knew I was going to be punished when I got home, so I prepared myself the best I could. When we walked into the house, my mom started yelling at my stepdad, while grabbing her crutches and making her way to the door. She screamed for me to get a move on and grabbed my hand so tightly that I could barely hear the cry escape my mouth.

"If you wanna cry, I'll give you something to cry about!" *You just did*, I thought. She screamed at me the whole way to the salon, and when we got there, the receptionist told her that was what I asked for. A blatant lie. I was mute; no words dared to form. I failed to muster the courage to defend myself yet again. She berated my stepdad, who then redirected his anger toward me. A vicious cycle repeating itself.

"Go kneel on the register until I tell you to get up," he roared. I knew he wouldn't tell me to get up until bedtime; I could already feel the pain searing through my knees from the old floral-patterned cast iron register. I dropped my head, walked to the register, faced the wall, and knelt. I was no stranger to the burn in my chest, threatening to expose my weakness, and the prickle in my nose as a lonely tear began to fall. I wiped at it quickly to avoid getting in further trouble for crying, but I wasn't quick enough.

I jumped at the sound of my stepdad's voice. "Now you've got tomorrow to kneel, too, since you wanna fucking cry about it." I could see my mom from the corner of my eye, looking at me with what appeared to be hate, and I wondered if she'd ever find it in her heart to love me again.

At bedtime, I prayed to God for just a few more hours than normal to be added to the day. I knew my dad would wake me up at six o'clock in the morning, and after my bowl of Kix, I'd go back on the register for the day. My knees already had the floral-pattern harshly imprinted into my skin, the bruising deepening in color. *It could be worse*, I thought. *We could have the thinly lined registers like in our old apartment that cut my knees.* As I laid in bed, my hand drifted from my sore knees to my chest, as if I could physically rub away the pain that lodged itself deep within my heart. I let my tears flow quietly, scared that if I cried too loudly, I'd wake up the monster within my stepdad.

When darkness fell, it was as though a weight descended upon me, heavier with each ticking second of the clock. Each moment that brought me closer to dawn felt like a step toward another battleground. This was a common phenomenon: when the activity and noise of the day died down, we could finally process the events and our feelings about the day. I found myself whispering prayers into the night, asking God for extra moments where I could escape into the haven of my thoughts, away from the reality that would greet me in the morning.

Right on time, my dad woke me up at six o'clock in the morning. I dragged myself out of bed. My body moved through the motions, but my soul was left somewhere between the sheets. Downstairs, a bowl of Kix awaited me; their bland taste offered little comfort. I sat across from my brother and saw the pain on his face, knowing these punishments were the only time he couldn't protect me. We exchanged a silent knowing, a moment of compassion, and then it was back to the register for the day—another day of kneeling, of plastering on a calm face, and of pretending.

In this vulnerable state, I realized safety in this moment meant survival. We often think of safety as a situation where someone is protecting us, like my brother did for me for so many years. Sometimes, for me, it was cradled between the agonies of yesterday and the uncertainties of the new day. Lying in my bed, I found a flicker of hope that refused to be extinguished, a whispered reminder from the depths of my spirit, a soft but resilient voice that said, "You're still here. You've survived, and you will continue to do so."

Yes, my knees may have been bruised, and my heart may have been fractured, but they were still functioning and still part of me. And if those battered parts of me could keep going, then so could the rest of me, because even in the night sky, the tiniest star can break through the overwhelming darkness.

Chapter 7

In The Spotlight

They say to belong is to find sanctuary, not in places or people, but within yourself. I had it backwards for most of my life, always focusing less on finding myself and more on seeking that elusive sanctuary within others. Searching high and low, never looking inward, always seeking outside counsel for validation and acceptance. The one rule of belonging was defied by me at every corner, even when the universe would attempt to steer me in the right direction.

My hunt for sanctuary started when I was eight. I felt draped in the deceptive comfort of innocence but weighed down by a growing desperation for approval. This is when my first bad habit was formed, on our back porch at 60 Summer Street in Newport. Surrounded by the eager eyes of my five friends and even my own brother, a cigarette lay before me, presenting a heavy and loaded implication. Their silent judgment produced palpable electricity in the air. "Just do it," they all said, not as a cheer but as a push towards compliance that promised social currency.

The sun started to dip, and it felt like an attempt to put me in the spotlight. The long shadows mingled with the evening air, as if mocking my weakness. The breeze was thick with the scent of youthful defiance and stolen treasures; a pack of cigarettes, a can of beer, and the tension of peer pressure.

"Come on, Lex," my brother nudged me, extending the cigarette as if it were a rite of passage. The unspoken message was clear: refusal was not an option. I would be the anomaly, the squeaky wheel, the pariah.

"I don't want to," I whispered, my voice frail, consumed by their anxious whispers and self-satisfied grins.

"Just do it. If you don't, you'll rat us all out," I heard one of the girls say. "Don't be a baby." I remember feeling panicked inside, not knowing if I took a drag of the cigarette if I'd die. *Would I not be able to stop coughing? Would I get caught?* The questions rolling through my mind were endless loops playing in my head. And then my subconscious started saying, *Just comply. If you do it, they'll like you. It'll be fine.*

It almost felt like there were options, but the choice wasn't really mine to make. *Was it?* My fingers reluctantly gripped the cigarette, its papery surface smooth against my fingertips. The spark of the lighter, the tobacco catching fire, the first drag, and the crackling sounds it made with the inhale of my breath. It felt harsh and hot, tearing through me. Yet, as the smoke swirled in my mouth and down into my underdeveloped lungs, it began to feel like a caress, a dangerous hug, a twisted form of acceptance. I exhaled, and the smoke danced in artful spirals. As if a performance of my hazardous belonging.

I became the star of that dimly lit porch, my youthful lungs undeterred by the toxic fumes. Before I could fully process the experience of my first time smoking, the beer followed, its bitterness clashing with the lingering taste of tobacco, sealing the deal on my ultimate surrender to do what everyone demanded of me. I belonged. But the questions that kept playing in my mind were: *At what cost? What's next?*

I was still constantly the square peg in a world of round holes, yearning for acceptance in a universe that seemed to have pre-decided my role based on external factors, especially at school. The hue of my skin, the threads that clung to my frame, and the fragments of a family that couldn't be pieced together marked me, depicting a picture that never truly told my story.

Beneath the surface, there was a smoldering ember that refused to be put out. An ember of hope that somewhere, someday, I'd find where I truly belonged. A place, a moment, or even a person who'd look beyond the superficial and recognize the soul that simply longed to be seen, heard, and loved.

By the age of ten, the school playground seemed like a smaller version of the world outside. The laughter, the cliques, and the unspoken rules all mimicked the larger world we would eventually have to navigate. But for me, that playground was both a haven and a battlefield.

Every day, like clockwork, the popular girls would gather around to jump rope. Their ponytails swung in rhythm with the rope, their laughter rising and falling like a melody. As if under a spell, I'd find myself gravitating towards them, silently wishing to be a part of that joyful circle. But they had an invisible barrier around them, and I was on the outside looking in.

Some could argue that kids can be cruel, but it's more likely they're mirroring the prejudices and biases of the world around them. So, every day, they'd notice me and point fingers; their whispers carried on the wind like a haunting warning, branding me as "weird" and "creepy." My presence seemed like a disruption to their perfect world.

On this particular crisp spring day, the atmosphere was thick with tension. The sky was a canvas of angry, swirling grays, reflecting the turmoil within me. The sun played hide and seek, giving me only brief moments of warmth. That warmth was a clear contrast to the chill I felt within and around me.

A cacophony of emotions filled my body on the playground: the prickles of sadness in my heart, full-body rage, and an awful sense of isolation. In that overwhelming moment, the only thing I wanted to do was find a way to scream a big "FUCK YOU" to the world.

Before I knew it, I found myself wandering farther into the field and away from the playground, distancing myself from the echoing laughter and intense mocking gazes. The farther I walked, the more the world seemed to blur around me.

In an act of rebellion, I pulled out a cigarette from my small black backpack that replicated a purse in its cutest form. The cigarette was a symbol, not of defiance but of a cry for acknowledgment or maybe even help. Lighting it up on the playground felt like an act of freedom. Freedom in choice, in not caring if I belonged, in making a decision for myself. I took a deep pull of that cigarette, feeling the burn of the smoke in my ten-year-old lungs, mixing with the storm of my emotions.

As the smoke wafted upwards, it seemed to carry away a part of my pain. It wasn't a solution, and it wasn't an escape. But for that fleeting moment, under the looming clouds in that limitless yet empty field, I felt a strange sense of closeness with the world. A realization that storms, both within and outside, can eventually pass.

The coils of smoke curling up from my cigarette were almost poetic in their dance, a symbol of my young rebellion against a world that had so often isolated me. But as fleeting and temporary as smoke, so was my moment of pause. And that day, destiny had other plans.

The hours that followed were a whirlwind of commotion, classes, and raging internal thoughts. The bus ride home seemed to hold an energy I hadn't really felt before. It was heavy, with a dash of anxiety, maybe. As I stood to dart off the bus like every other day, I was too in my head to realize the little black bag occupying the seat I once sat in. That forgotten bag on the bus was the first time I recognized my shape-shifting abilities—or more aptly, *acting* abilities.

When I finally made it home, I found my mom on the phone.

"Oh, I'll be having a talk with her; you better fucking believe that!" I only caught the tail end of the conversation, but I knew I was the only other "she" in the house. The loud crash of the phone meeting the receiver signaled I was about to meet a version of her I wouldn't like. Mom's stern face could have eaten a hole through my face had I not looked away when I did. *Who was that, and what did I do so badly to make her that angry?* My heart raced, each beat echoing the rapid thoughts running through my head. Slight trembles formed throughout my body as I prepared for the wrath I was about to face.

She charged at me, ripping my backpack off my shoulder to yank it open, breaking the zipper in the process. Mom dumped all the contents out, right there on the floor.

"Where are they, Alex?" she demanded. Alex is the name she would call me when she was angry. Most often, it was used to compare me to my father, a man I never remembered meeting. She must have gauged the look on my face that silently said, "What are 'they?'" Every possible scenario ran through my mind, and I couldn't figure out what she was talking about. Then she said the words that gutted me from the inside out.

"The fucking cigarettes," she spat. "Don't play stupid; you know what I'm talking about, you little bitch." Only my gasp was audible after that—not because of the insults she threw my way but because of the fear filling my entire body. I stood in silence, not saying anything, just looking at her blankly. *How did she or anyone else even know?*

Those cigarettes—Camel non-filters, full-flavor shorts—were my stepdad's signature brand. He'd leave packs carelessly around, and I had taken advantage of this oversight. Or at least I thought I did. The Salt-N-Pepa cassette tape case seemed like the perfect hideaway, a relic of another era that no one would bother with. But now that its contents were exposed, I was trapped in the spotlight and didn't see a way out. When my stepdad got home about thirty minutes later, my mom told him what the school said. When he yanked my arm toward the door, I held back the prickle of tears threatening to expose my fear, confirmation, and punishment. That was the longest ten-minute drive I ever experienced, and when we pulled into the school parking lot, every sweat gland was working overtime. *This is it for me. I am about to be destroyed, annihilated, and probably die before I make it back home.*

My mom, stepdad, and I walked through those ugly forest green doors with a purpose. My dad grasped my arm so tightly that I thought it might break off. He barged into the principal's office and sat me down so hard in that dark blue plastic chair outside the door that it screeched as it slid backwards. The principal's office had always seemed intimidating, but never more than in that moment. The walls suffocated me, the silence interrupted only by the constant ringing of the office phone at the receptionist's desk and voices that sounded like low murmurs on the other side of the wall as my mother and stepdad were informed of all the details. The weight of the impending consequences pressed heavily on my chest. All I wanted to do was run, but I had nowhere to go.

"Penny, Vinny, we found a Camel filter cigarette in your daughter's bag, as I stated on the phone. She wa—" I was handed a lifeline, unexpected but welcomed. The word "filter"—one simple and seemingly insignificant word—was my saving grace. The principal misspoke. Saying it was a non-filtered cigarette meant my dad wouldn't think it was his; he only smoked non-filtered cigarettes. This small mistake, the slight difference in wording, was enough to sow doubt into his mind and give me ammo to perform like I was being nominated for an Emmy or even an Oscar! All I knew was that I intended to give the performance of a lifetime.

Sometimes desperation gives birth to creativity; at least it did for me. I quickly spun a tale, pinning the blame on a girl named Abigail, one of the school's troublemakers. My stepdad, ever perceptive, shot me a glance that pierced right through my act. It was a gaze filled with knowledge and understanding, one that said, "I know the truth, but let's see how this plays out for you." I doubled down, tears flowing, playing on the sad, asthmatic girl that I was. The sheer absurdity of an asthmatic kid smoking was my final play.

"Why would I smoke when I know it can kill me?" I blubbered. "It doesn't make any sense that you would believe that those were mine. It had to have been Abigail either setting me up or being scared to get caught. It was her; I know it was!"

Those words seem to have worked, or maybe it was the tears. Before I knew it, the principal was apologizing to my parents for the misunderstanding and for dragging them to the school. My mom's rage seemed to simmer, but my stepdad kept a side eye. I didn't care whether it was a genuine belief or a lack of concern—I was let off the hook. No suspension, no expulsion, no grounding, just the terrifying gaze of my stepdad. The world outside the principal's office had never seemed brighter than in that moment. When we left the school, I marveled at the sky, which had never been clearer. It's funny that just hours before that moment, the sky was dancing with storm clouds, and then, just like my internal feelings, it was clear. *For now.*

More than relief, that day imparted a lesson, proof of the unpredictable nature of life and the unexpected turns it can take. It also taught me that if I mold into shapes and characters that appeal to others, I can manipulate my misfortune into something I can control. That was a feeling I liked, and that was the moment my people-pleasing, perfectionism, and performances truly began. I wanted more of that feeling of control.

Chapter 8

A Selfish Decision

A FEW YEARS after the smoking incident and the separation of my mom and stepdad, my sense of control was lost again. As sirens blared, my heart shattered. Life as I knew it was about to change forever. The only person who protected me from all the evil in life was being taken away from me.

This was the day my brother was taken away, and it's etched in my memory like a scar that refuses to fade. I was thirteen and he was fifteen—still kids, trying to navigate a world that often felt unforgiving to people like us. The sound of the handcuffs clicking around his wrists was deafening, reverberating in my ears long after he was led away. Rage filled every fiber of my body as I screamed at the police officer, "WHY?! He didn't do anything!"

That moment was a freeze-frame, a horrible snapshot in time that I couldn't escape. As the officer spoke, I could only hear muffled sounds, not words, as I watched the motion of his lips moving. The room closed in on me. My heartbeat became the only sound I could hear. Panicked, I screamed again, "Let him go, you asshole!" My mom's lips were moving now, but I couldn't make out the sounds, nor could I figure out who she was talking to. I searched Shawn's eyes for even the slightest hint of what I should do next, how I should navigate life, and how I could protect him. I was met with fear, shame, and confusion.

A few days after he was arrested, he called me. My heart sank when I heard the robotic voice through the phone—that standard, soul-crushing recording: "This is a collect call from inmate Shawn Gardner at the Northern State Correctional Facility. All calls from inmates are recorded. Press zero to accept this call..." My finger hovered over the zero with a mix of anxiety and urgency. I pressed zero for the third time since he'd been incarcerated.

I was greeted with Shawn's voice. The voice that was my guiding light, the hope I carried, and my safety. But this time it was tinged with fear and uncertainty, and his anxiousness flooded my ears. He started talking so fast that I had to focus hard on what he was saying.

"I have a choice: take a plea deal and come home in a couple of days, or go to trial and risk it all." The words came out so fast, it felt like they punched me in the gut. His next question would be the question I'd regret answering for the rest of my life. "What should I do, Lex?" At that moment, my thoughts were selfish. I missed him so badly; he was my protector, my rock, and my best friend. The thought of not having him around was unbearable.

"Take the deal" flew out of my mouth so fast I had to take a beat to realize what I'd actually said. I just repeated, "Come home, Shawny. Please, just come home! I can't do this without you here." My desperation couldn't be hidden.

No matter how many times the evidence would later say he was innocent, the damage was already done. My brother and I had always been each other's confidants, a support system in a world that seemed intent on tearing us down. On this particular day, I wish he hadn't come to me for my *stupid* advice.

What if he had fought? What if he had cleared his name right then and there instead of carrying the weight of a criminal record and a sentence that took his young adulthood for a crime he didn't commit? I'll never know, and that guilt is something I carry with me every single day.

Despite the pain and regret I felt, Shawn never blamed me, and we continued to be extremely close. Well, as close as you can be to an inmate. We leaned on each other even more in the years that followed, our bond unbreakable even when tested by the most severe strains. Still, I can't help but look back at that pivotal moment, pondering the "what if's" and "if onlys" that continue to swirl in my mind.

As I navigate life's complexities, I'm reminded that the choices we make can reverberate far beyond the moments in which they are made. Sometimes, in trying to protect the ones we love, we end up causing them more harm. It's a lesson learned in the hardest way possible, and one I will never forget.

The promise that my brother would come home turned out to be a bitter lie. He remained behind bars for five years, only to return several more times throughout his short life. All while the world as I knew it began to disintegrate. So many questions buzzed, creating tension in our already troubled house. Guilt gnawed at me daily, but I said nothing, sinking deeper into a destructive, silent depression.

In the wake of my brother's extended absence, I spiraled. I drank more, smoked more, and lost myself in a haze of poor choices and company I should have avoided. When Shawn discovered this, he was livid. He yelled at me, then slammed the phone and didn't speak to me for six agonizing months. His silence was both an absence and a presence; every tick of the clock served as a reminder of the rift between us.

Life inside the prison was no walk in the park for Shawn. Within the first month, he was ruthlessly bullied, a bucket of urine was dumped over his head, his belongings were stolen, and there was even a stabbing attempt. Every time the phone rang, my heart leaped into my throat, and I feared the worst. I didn't know what anxiety was back then, but it consumed me. The one person who had always protected me, who had always been there, was now unreachable, locked behind bars, and in dangerous situations all alone.

But every Saturday, like clockwork, Mom and I would visit him. Those visits were slices of the past; moments stolen from a reality we could no longer fully inhabit. We'd talk, play cards, and, inevitably, we'd cry. The tears felt like more than just water; they were more like bits of our soul leaking because the pain of keeping everything inside was too great to bear.

If I could turn back the hands of time, I would have told him to fight. I would have urged him to not take that plea deal, to stand strong, and to face the storm. Because maybe, just maybe, he would have won. He would be free, unburdened by a criminal record, and our lives would have taken a different path. But time is unforgiving, and all I can do now is learn from those painful lessons and hope those who hear my story do, too.

I'm learning—slowly, painfully—to forgive myself and to make peace with the choices that can't be undone. For Shawn, for myself, and for the fragile hope that even when life fractures us into a million pieces, it also gives us the courage to put ourselves back together, one tiny shard at a time.

Chapter 9

Deception

The situation with Shawn caused me to lose faith in myself and others, and I became vulnerable to the influences of others. Experiences in life can take you on a path of loneliness, uncertainty, and feeling as if you don't know yourself. I began to shield myself from the world around me, and when I did, bits and pieces of me began to feel lost. There were parts of me that had been stolen from me at fifteen. Someone else's view and opinion made me think that no matter what happened to me, I wasn't worth listening to and I was not believed; I started living into the stigmas placed on me. It was a heavy feeling that no one would ever truly know me, and frankly, I didn't know that anyone would have wanted to. The world has been cruel and cold toward me, but I've learned to keep fighting. Every day, I put my armor on and prepare for battle. The problem is that everyone became my enemy, especially me.

It's a constant battle to seek friendly faces and gauge others' body language to ensure we are saying and doing the right things, whether to impress our family or anyone else. For some of us, that means tucking who we really are away so the world can't see us shape-shifting into different people, molding into the environments around us. Following suit with things that don't actually serve us or the persona we want to be. And what's worse is when something devastating happens to you and there's no one who believes you, and it's someone you know and trust who hurts you. When I was fifteen, I learned the hard way that even when someone says they are your friend, they will still take things from you that certainly aren't theirs to take. And what's worse is when someone else feels the same way you do but will still leave you to get eaten alive by the wolves who will surely come.

It was a typical cold day in January 2002 at the local Newport skating rink, where you would find all of us fifteen- and sixteen-year-olds after school. I wore my jeans pulled over stained white figure skates, a sweater, gloves, and hat and pretended I wasn't freezing my ass off, but hey, it was the cool thing to do. I remember this night starting with so much laughter and excitement for the remainder of the school year and how many more nights we would get at the skating rink.

You know that feeling when you find a place where you feel like you belong and find yourself laughing at almost anything? That's the joy I felt at the skating rink, surrounded by people I believed cared for me. On this day, everything started the same, until the metallic greenish-teal Cavalier showed up. The driver was someone I used to get excited about seeing, one of my best friends, Kevin. He was someone I felt safe around.

That night, my girlfriend Lisa, Kevin, and I decided to go for a ride and smoke a cigarette, as we'd done before. The conversation was different that night. We talked about flirty things, made comments about each other, and laughed. We were having lighthearted fun, joking around—this was a safe place. *Right?*

As the car looped behind what was Shaw's Grocery Store at the time, my stomach turned. I knew something was wrong when he stopped the car and put it in park. I had that feeling in the pit of my stomach that instinctually said something bad was about to happen. The way he looked back at Lisa and me in the backseat exposed a darkness in his eyes. It was different, scary, and demanding.

He started making comments about our "pink tacos" and how hot we were, making a hand gesture while saying, "Two for the pink, one for the stink." I had no idea what that meant, but when he held up his hand, displaying the gesture, it made me sick to my stomach. Mentally, as a woman, I had prepared for a moment like this. I always told myself I would run, fight, and get out of the situation, but in that very moment I was frozen in time, numb, silent, and still. I now understood what paralysis from fear felt like. The trust I once had for this person was ripped away, and I didn't feel anything but shame, regret, and disgust for myself. Never feeling so lonely, never feeling so exposed, and gutted as I did in that very moment.

"You can't just tease a guy and expect to walk away without doing anything," he said, looking at me in the rear-view mirror. The dome light came on as he opened the driver-side door and stepped out of the car. I looked at my friend, whose face matched my panicked feeling. "I don't want to do anything; I just want to go back to the skating rink. Let's just go," I begged, panic rising in my chest. "Please!"

This feeling of not being able to escape someone else's control was overwhelming. I sat there as he planned to take the last of my innocence. The ripple effect that would come from this assault was unbeknownst to me at the time, but it would surely affect me for the rest of my teen years and into adulthood. The trust I once had in a safe space disappeared, and the trauma set in when he carelessly took the last of my sweet soul. No one was there to protect me; no one was there to care; only judgment and shame remained. I felt dirty and wanted to remove my own skin, which now crawled with self-resentment. I felt stained and used in a way I can't explain; it's just a feeling of sickness, pain, worry, and anger all rolled into one.

I was always good at escaping in my mind, dissociating; it would shut down and take me to the most beautiful places. But this time there was nothing; the field of lilacs and lavender flowers and the trees and fields with the most magical shades of purple didn't reveal themselves. No bliss, no haven, just fear. I just wanted the feeling of sunshine on my face and to be free from everyone and everything—an escape only I could experience, even if the outside reflected darkness in the sky and streets of snow. My mind was my place of protection until that night. The absence of escape felt like betrayal. I was the best at abandoning myself in any time of need. Rage washed over me as I criticized myself for not fighting and protecting myself.

"Let's just go." The panic in Lisa's voice snapped me back to reality. As we tried to get the seat moved forward to open the passenger side door of the two-door vehicle, Kevin moved the opposite seat forward, blocking my only alternative exit. He began climbing in the back and placed his hand on my upper thigh, leaning forward to slam the door closed. When he turned around, I was met with that devilish stare, only inches away from one another. His laugh taunted me.

Paralysis washed over me as he moved to the middle of the back seat, closing the distance between my friend and me. Tense and scared, I felt my heart pounding against my chest so hard that I thought it might actually escape my body. Frozen, defenseless, a coward who couldn't protect herself. As his hand began traveling, exploring our bodies, I went numb, frozen in time like a preserved fossil, meant to be in a different time and place—not here, not in this moment being touched against my will. I remember him moving my body around, touching my virgin body in ways it wasn't supposed to be touched.

"No, I don't want to do this," I said for the fourth time, this time just a whimper. Tears rolled down my cheeks. I felt disgusting and dirty as he forced and coerced my movement—he clearly knew how to get what he wanted. He moved my head in directions I didn't want to go, but the more I resisted, the harder he would push, eventually winning the battle. I held my breath, wishing I was dead rather than there.

After what felt like a lifetime, he was trying to pull my pants down when a car drove up behind us. They slowed as they passed, seemingly unable to see what was going on inside. It must have spooked him.

"You can't tell anyone about this," he commanded, wild-eyed. "You're fifteen, and I can get into serious trouble. You don't want to ruin my military career, do you?" He was in my face, pointing now. "DO YOU?!" I was mute, but the boom of his voice startled me. I nodded my head urgently in agreement.

My hands trembled as I found the buttons on my pants to fasten them, thanking God for the car that passed. The velvety fabric beneath my hands on the back seat felt tainted with sin. A place that was once comforting and safe turned into the scene of my nightmares. Literally.

We returned to the skating rink, and all three of us were quiet until Kevin grabbed my arm to stop me before I could exit the car. Panic rose in my chest.

"You'll tell no one," he threatened, looking deep into my eyes to reinforce his warning. "Do you understand me?"

"No one," I forced out of my mouth, mostly to break free of his grasp. Then, I scurried as quickly as I could out of the car, finally taking the breath I'd been holding in my lungs. People were talking to me, but I had no idea what was being said. I could only replay it over and over in my head. Every word was muffled, as if they were talking under water, or maybe I was under water, drowning. Someone asked if I was okay, and I remember walking to the bathroom and staying there for quite a while, crying from the shame I felt inside. *How could I let this happen? How could I not fight back? How could I be so fucking weak?* I kept repeating, *You're disgusting, Alexis.*

When I came out twenty or maybe thirty minutes later, my mom was coming down the road, screaming my name. As she got closer to the skating rink, her voice was filled with rage. Once she was just about to me, she asked, "Were you raped or touched?" I looked around and saw my friend Lisa on the pay phone, crying to someone, and I knew at that moment the truth had been exposed. Remembering his words, *"You'll tell no one,"* came back in a rush to haunt me. She asked again and then said, "Some girl called the police, Alexis. They said you were raped."

"No. I don't know what you're talking about."

"If I find out you're out here being a whore," she shook her head, "you're going to be sorry."

When we got home, I wanted to take a shower, but my mom wouldn't allow me to. So, as she followed me around the house, calling me names and accusing me of being a whore, I just gently closed my bedroom door and wrapped my blankets as tight as I could around me. Protecting myself from the outside. At that moment, I knew I was safe with no one. No one would protect me from the evil in the world, and even when something terrible happens, it is my fault.

The next morning, a cop was at my bedroom door, asking me to go downstairs and answer some questions about the night before. I hesitantly followed him to the kitchen table and sat down, not making eye contact.

"If something happened to you, you need to tell us. I need your honesty here," he said, sitting across from me at the kitchen table. I was in shock, scared of what would happen if I told.

I feigned ignorance. "I don't know what you're talking about."

"Are you sure?"

"Nothing happened." I tried my best to sound convincing. Then, they told me there was another girl at the skating rink who called it into someone else, and that person called the police. She told them what happened, and they now needed my story to corroborate. I still didn't want to speak, remembering Kevin's warning. *I can't tell them.*

My mom pulled me into her bedroom and pushed me against the door. She screamed in my face that I was a whore. Her words cut deep into my soul, stinging the open wound of something I couldn't even comprehend. That's when it happened.

"Fine!" I screamed back, defeated. "I'll tell you! He made us kiss him, touch him with our hands and mouths, and he touched us in our private areas. I'm a virgin. I've never done anything before; it hurt, and it was scary. Are you happy now that you know? I'm a big whore because someone took advantage of me. He didn't have sex with us because a car went by, scaring him."

She swung the door open, stormed past me, and retrieved the officer. I was asked to repeat everything I just spoke aloud, the punishment that would surely come looming over my head. He looked at me questioningly, as if I had made it up, even though he had pushed for my confession. His disbelief was only more evidence to protect myself and trust no one. Shame spread throughout my entire body. I felt exposed, unheard, and now terrified that I told Kevin's secret, and the police didn't believe me anyway.

The rest of that day went by in a blur, from the hospital to undergo a sexual assault forensic exam, to the police station giving my statement of events over and over, to my discussion with a victims' advocate. But with every person I spoke to, I could see their skepticism of my story. They didn't believe me. I knew it was only a matter of time before they called him in, and we'd go over it again. The only problem was that when they called him in, he didn't speak. He said, "You have no evidence; this girl is just trying to get me in trouble." *I guess being a sergeant in the military gives you credibility, and being the black girl in a white town gets you the stereotype of being a liar, troublemaker, or just asking for it.* I internalized what I learned from this situation: I deserved it, too. All these tallies of bad experiences equaled bad consequences for me.

I had to do mandatory counseling. My assigned counselor asked me a lot of the same questions the cops did, and I answered them. Her last question was, "He stated you threw yourself at him and wanted it. Do you think maybe you led him on and brought this on yourself?" At that moment, I vowed to never speak about it again. I knew it didn't matter what I said; I would always be the reason someone else did something wrong to me.

I began having nightmares about Kevin and his friends coming into my house in the middle of the night, putting a cloth over my mouth that would make me pass out, and when I would wake next, I was in the woods naked, tied up to stakes on the ground, and splayed in the most exposing way. When I came to, I'd try pulling against the restraints while he and his friends would laugh. "You're not going anywhere, you little bitch." He'd say. "I'm going to finish what I started." That's when he'd press a cold blade against my thigh, applying enough pressure to draw blood.

My muffled screams went unheard as their laughing got louder and louder. In the nightmare, I could terrifyingly and undeniably feel the searing pain as he thrust the knife inside me, then removed it only to begin cutting my face and my arms. My flesh was covered in blood as he and his friends took turns using me, calling me a whore, a little bitch, and slowly killing me. For over two years, I had this same nightmare, waking up in panic, sweating in fear, and grabbing at my body, looking for evidence of it being a reality. I never wanted to sleep and face that demon. Exhaustion would always win and take over, repeating this nightmare every night, waking just before my last breath would leave my body.

Every morning, like clockwork, I would walk the two miles to the high school. I'd often see Kevin and his friends driving around in the car, which haunted my memories. Driving fast and honking down the streets, yelling things out the window, and revving their engine—a constant reminder of how exposed I was in the streets. On several occasions, they almost hit me. I'd call the "victims' advocate," and they would conveniently say there was nothing they could do. But it felt more like there was nothing they were *willing* to do for *me*.

Lisa, who originally called the cops, exposing us both, decided she would not cooperate anymore, but there was no turning back for me. I'd spoken my truth. She abandoned me in a situation she placed me in by telling someone, and I became the liar and target for revenge. Everyone in school found out; it was devastating. Several mornings, I walked to my locker to find the word "whore" written in big, bold letters with red lipstick. I swiped my finger through it and watched the smeared line expand onto the next locker. Standing there in humiliation and dread, I wanted to disappear. Words written on a locker cut deeper than I knew possible. Hit in the face with things thrown in my direction and being tripped—sometimes down the stairs —became my new reality. A reality that had me slowly slipping away. Falling into a black hole of depression, anxiety, and suffering. No one to turn to, no one who believed me, and I couldn't escape being "the whore;" not at home and certainly not at school.

This was a pivotal time for me. I began drinking heavily. It didn't matter what the drink was; if I could get my hands on it, I'd drink it. Luckily for me, my stepdad always had beer and vodka stocked at his apartment and I had access to tequila or Bacardi at my neighbor's house. Every drink was a prayer for no more suffering; I wanted the nightmares to stop, and I wanted everyone in school to disappear so I could just live in a world by myself. I thought of death a lot back then. It's amazing how you can smile enough that no one questions a thing. I realized if I faked being happy for long enough, people stopped checking in, asking questions, or caring. It was like the universe was saying, "You're on your own, kid." I was told to figure it out, don't tell anyone, and keep your fucking legs closed. Life was crashing down on me from every direction, but somehow, I kept pushing through. Even when I didn't want to. Even when the only thing that sounded like peace was ending it all.

Every guy I'd encounter after that became a trigger. I never knew what they would want to take from me. I only operated in fear, never fully trusting anyone who crossed my path. I lost my virginity a few months after the incident. Not because I was hopelessly in love or really wanted to experience the world of sex, but because I was so afraid of something being taken, afraid of living through another nightmare.

A couple of girlfriends and I went out riding around with some guys they knew. I was in the front seat since they were all pretty much locking lips like life depended on it in the back seat. I remember feeling the heat from his hand on my knee; my whole body went rigid from my head to my toes. As he got more comfortable, his hand navigated to my thigh, and the lack of response from me was like a silent confirmation. I knew what came next.

My brain immediately flickered to the back seat of Kevin's car. The stares of everyone who told me I brought it onto myself flashed in my head. I wanted to exit my own skin. It was terrible. People talked about sex like it was amazing, but it hurt, it felt disgusting, and I could feel the shame once again building with every minute until it fully engulfed me, swallowing me whole. It didn't last long, thank God, but long enough for me to be triggered into a spiral.

Every sixty-eight seconds, a woman, child, or man is sexually assaulted *in the United States*, according to data from the Rape, Abuse, & Incest National Network (RAINN). Just Americans—imagine what that data would be across the globe. No one should ever be degraded by experiences that feel as if a piece of our soul is taken from us. Being set up for failure and lifelong trauma without warning, and further, in the case of many, without a plan to work through it, is hard to cope with. My assigned counselor was a brutal reminder that no blame could be shed on the monster who haunts my dreams; rather, I, the victim, should be ashamed for letting such a thing happen.

Chapter 10

This Isn't A Hallmark Movie

I thought growing up in a small town would be a beautiful thing. You know, like what you see in all the Lifetime and Hallmark movies. Tight-knit communities, cozy coffee shops, and picturesque main streets, resulting in the charm of a small town. But the small town of Newport, Vermont, felt suffocating most of the time. No one really knew me or cared to know me, especially being a freshman in high school. After the assault and its "investigation," I endured years of harassment, stuck in the same place. Having no hope of breaking free was depressing.

Like tires in the mud, the more I spun my wheels, the faster I got nowhere. The analogy of rocks flying in my direction was so fitting at the time. I was constantly labeled "whore," "liar," "nigger," and so on, and further, by the very people who had known me since I was a little girl. It was like living in an echo chamber—everyone's racist and misogynistic opinions influenced and validated others' opinions of me. The vision of what my life would look like often made my classmates laugh at my audacity to dream about the possibilities outside of this place.

Most kids talked about the college they wanted to go to or starting a family, but everything in me was filled with wonder and adventure. That was one blessing I could take from my childhood: my sense of imagination and endless dreams created an urge to travel and explore. I wanted to know if there were more people like me who had experienced a lot of shit in life but fought to stay above water.

Like many other times in my life, I sought places in the world that told me I belonged, but it was more like trying to figure out a damn Rubik's cube. Never knowing what color goes where, what pattern or shape to take, who truly sees *me*, and who sees me as an *opportunity*. The more I tried to convince myself that I could trust people, the more evidence that I wasn't worth anyone's time would appear. I guess I was just another black girl caught in a system that was not designed to protect me.

So often I felt like I was swimming in an ocean of people with no one to help me, even when I was drowning. It felt like I was invisible; my desires and dreams sank to the bottom of the sea, swallowed whole by the currents of life. Society had already written me off as a tattoo of judgment that I couldn't wash away in that town, and believe me, I felt it.

I was cold-shouldered by an adult—someone's mother, to be exact. Since the rumor about my assault surfaced, this mom told her daughter Sara, right in front of me, that she couldn't hang out with me because I was a "prostitute." My mouth fell open with shock, humiliation, and disbelief. I was sitting on a set of stairs beside my mom and her boyfriend, and this woman *still* labeled me a prostitute. I'd been called a lot of things, but a prostitute, *never!* I don't know if it was because I was wearing a tank top, a jean skirt, and heels, or if this lady was just crazy. I loved those dark brown, open-toed, lace heels. But to that mother, my outfit was nothing but a red flag—an invitation to label and judge me. *Why would she think that about me?* Her words cut into my soul, questioning everything she was seeing through a lens of judgment I couldn't comprehend.

The worst part was how I let this lady tear me down, and then I tried to plead with her.

"I'm only out here with my mom because I'm grounded, and this is the building my mom's boyfriend lives in." I pointed at the building and then at my mom, sitting on the steps. "I'm no trouble at all. I swear." My frizzy curls swayed back and forth as I spoke with emphasis, on a mission to prove I wasn't the despicable words she spoke over me. She just rolled her eyes, not believing me, looking at my mom with distrust.

"I'm sure that's your pimp over there, and my daughter is not getting caught up in any of that shit with you." Her finger pierced my heart every time she vigorously pointed in my face and then toward my mom's boyfriend. He was a Latino man with slicked back hair, tan skin, a leather jacket, and a cane. I knew how it looked, but it wasn't the scenario she'd imagined. It was simply a stereotype taken too far. I was grounded, and my mom made me go everywhere she did unless I was working. This was her way of making sure I didn't get in trouble. All the more reason for this woman to believe me. Looking back, I can see people never truly saw who I was or the person I'd wanted to be—just the scrappy girl who longed for more.

Desire is such a wild thing. You never know if you can make it happen. For the better part of my life, I believed my needs and wants were not even on the radar. It didn't matter what I wanted or who I thought I could be. In my head, I would always only amount to the girl others saw: a druggy, alcoholic whore who'd live on welfare for the rest of her life.

I kept asking, *God, when will I live up to this feeling I have inside? When will you show me the way? Am I going to be worthless forever? Will I end up on the streets and become a drug addict? What will life look like for me in the future?*

I've already lived through so many dark times. I would plead to God, *Lord, I need you to show me the light. I don't think I can do this much longer.*

When I felt no answers to my prayers, I asked, *When will life be fair? When will the world see me for who I really am? When will I feel happiness that is truly my own?*

Questions constantly flooded my mind, each one tethered to a desperation that I couldn't shake. Each question was a plea, an outpouring of my innermost fears and longings. But they felt less like a prayer and more like a guttural shout into an empty void. My own questions echoed back to me, not the answers I sought.

So there I was, just months shy of turning sixteen, standing at the intersection of who I was and who the world said I should be, wrestling with the dread, heartache, and pain that had been my constant companions. I could only wonder: *When will I finally live the life that's been silently burning inside me? When will God, or the universe, or whatever force governs this chaotic world, show me the way?*

I made a vow to myself—a sacred promise—that became my life's mantra. I would leave. I would escape this prison that some called home. Vermont and the small-mindedness, the judgments, the entire bubble that had tried to suffocate me. And I would *never* look back.

So, I let the people who tried to break me become the stepping stones on my path to something far greater. Their judgments, their disdain, and their ugly words would all be turned into a relentless drive for success. I would use every scrape and every scar as kindling for the fire that would light my way to something magnificent.

Chapter 11

The Reflection Is Ugly

I WAS SIXTEEN YEARS OLD, and this would be a whole new way of navigating life alone. For the first time, I was realizing that I was truly doing it all on my own. To cope, I found ways to rebel, project my anger, and lash out at whoever I could. My body became an easy target, feeling disgusted with my body. It was a constant reminder that the flaw was *me*.

For years, I fought the invisible war—a relentless battle against my own body. If I'm being one hundred percent honest, I still struggle with food. I eat when I'm happy, sad, or mad, and not usually in a healthy way to fuel my body. It was usually a moment of needing to feel numb. I'm certainly not in the same place I was when I'd abuse my body, constantly destroying myself to feel something—anything at all—but I do have to work every day to genuinely appreciate the body God so graciously granted me. Like anything else, some days are better than others.

The dinner table was always a hard place for me to be. Reminded of when my stepdad had the rule: everyone had to eat everything on their plate, and no drinks were permitted until after the food was gone. Even though he was no longer there, I found myself continuing the harsh torture, forcing down food I knew I didn't want to eat. The war waged in my heart as I'd cringe with every bite, wondering if I'd throw it up later or workout so hard I'd burn every damn calorie. It still makes me flinch knowing how cruel I was toward myself, especially in these moments where I was buried in a lack of self-worth and shame.

According to my peers and my mom, I was either "too fat" or "too skinny." Never just right or beautiful in my skin. I was the curvy girl with a big booty, and I assure you that was not a good thing in the nineties. Their words would echo in my ears, haunting my reflection in every mirror and distorting how I saw myself until I couldn't see anything but flaws.

There were days when I would avoid food like it was poison. My stomach would growl, pleading for nourishment, but I would tell myself that hunger was just another word for weakness. And then the pendulum would swing in the other direction: I would binge eat until I felt sick, full to the brim with regret and self-loathing.

The sun would have barely risen, and I would be on the floor, grinding out five hundred sit-ups. Then another five hundred before bed—a ritualistic punishment and desperate attempt to carve out a version of myself that could be lovable. Soon, five hundred wasn't enough. It escalated to seven hundred in the morning and seven hundred at night. It was as if each sit-up could somehow atone for the imperfections I saw in myself, as if I could sculpt away my self-doubt with every crunch.

As I tortured myself, I kept running from the truth. I was digging a hole so deep that I could barely see the light anymore.

My health started to falter; I felt weak, shaky, and constantly fatigued. I was starving, but more importantly, I was starving my soul of the love and acceptance it deserved.

Here's where I found the remedy: I stopped playing the game. I realized the only way out of this deathly cycle was to go through the pain. I started ignoring the societal norms, the judgmental glances, and the passive-aggressive comments; I could see through it. *I decided that what mattered most was how I saw myself.* I realized that my health and my happiness were internal things. Yes, external environments and the energy of others might have an influence, but I have a choice to either give in or move out of their reach.

I've begun tuning out the noise and focusing on *not* giving my power away to undeserving critics. No one has the right to determine my worth based on their perception of my body. I've come to see the judgments of others as reflections of their own insecurities and flaws. I'm learning to love my body as it is, standing firm against anyone who dares suggest I should feel otherwise. I remind myself that my body has carried me through every hardship and even given life. I'm learning to honor it for what it is: a marvel of nature deserving of love and care.

These days, the devil needs to try much harder than to throw a few comments my way because the plan God laid out for me is bigger than I can even imagine.

This is the power of God, saying He made me perfectly in His image. Should I go against God or tune out the haters and embrace every last inch of my precious body? I only get one, and I'll be damned if I go through my whole life ungrateful for it. Our vessels are one of our most extraordinary blessings; our bodies allow us to experience life.

Healing is a winding road, filled with setbacks and victories. It has been a tortuous journey to acknowledge that I have been my own worst enemy, locked in a toxic dance with societal expectations and deeply-rooted emotional wounds. Even today, I catch myself slipping into old patterns of thought, berating myself for my body's natural changes—especially as a mother and as I age. I'm building the courage to challenge those thoughts and to recognize that the face looking back at me in the mirror is not a blend of imperfections but a resilient survivor.

For my children, for my future, and for the peace and happiness that have been elusive for so long, I owe it to myself to try. This book has been a part of that transformation in rewriting my story, holding onto the power of voicing my fears, writing them down, and creating a new perspective.

Let's face it, the world has an infuriating double standard: if you're a mother who doesn't love every stretch mark or loose patch of skin, you're deemed ungrateful, as if you don't deserve the incredible gift of your children. But if you dare to embrace your changed body and flaunt your post-baby self with pride, society recoils, labeling you as "letting yourself go" or even going as far as calling you disgusting.

If I could go back and tell fifteen-year-old Alexis anything, it would be, "You are not your circumstance. Your circumstances are only a moment in time—even when it feels really big. You will be okay. You'll learn to navigate life in a healthier way; just look inside yourself and start to process all the negative thoughts you're fighting. When you do, you'll begin to heal much faster."

Healing is not linear. My journey is a path filled with setbacks, victories, tears and laughter, and despair and hope. But what's important is that it's *my* path, my truth, and one I navigate through fire and still emerge, not unscathed but certainly stronger.

My goal is to reach a state of contentment so profound that external judgments can't touch me. It's an ambitious aim, and I'm not there yet, but every step I take is a commitment to loving the perfectly imperfect body I have. I will keep dismissing the world's right to judge me, and, rather, hold on to the love that God has around me. All of this means the enemy is trying to hold me back from reaching my purpose, but I will with God's protection. After all, He did say, "They will wield weapons against you, but they shall not prosper." *Amen to that!*

Chapter 12

I'll Pretend To Be Your Juliet

IRONICALLY, I became friends with Sara. Yup, the one whose mom called me a prostitute. It truly felt like I scored a point against her mom, and I thought, *I'll show her.* Have you heard the saying, "We accept what we believe we deserve?" At the time, I thought I deserved whatever kind of love or friendship I could get, even if it wasn't real. My identity started to feel like a collage pieced together by desperation and the need for approval. I mastered the art of blending in so well that the girl staring back at me in the mirror was hardly recognizable.

I was tired. Tired of feeling like that jumbled collage bootstrapped together, I studied all the popular girls at school. The obvious thing to do, *duh*. I mean, it felt weird observing how they walked, how they talked, the clothes they wore, and whatever, but this became a subject I quickly excelled in, unlike my academic classes. My efforts to fit in went so far that I let Sara straighten my hair and plaster on some makeup. She said I would look beautiful like her. She layered on the makeup in her own shades—those meant for her porcelain skin.

I was so freaking excited to see the final product. A feeling washed over me that matched my inner glow. When I got to school, however, I realized I was more of a mess than without Sara's makeover. Her foundation made my face white, creating the impression that I wanted to be white. More makeup was smeared on my face than I initially realized. I looked like a reject from a beauty pageant gone wrong. And everyone certainly noticed. It was such a disaster that I wondered if she made me look like the living dead on purpose.

I just wanted to fit in with the cool kids. I wanted to be the funniest person at the table, with everyone laughing at my jokes. Instead, I admired them having fun interactions every day and wondered what kinds of conversations they were having. I wholeheartedly felt one day I'd be a part of it; I just didn't know how or when.

It wasn't until about a month later that I'd get my second chance. My neighbor, Sara, asked if I could drive her and a few others to the store. Dumbfounded and in shock, I shook my head up and down. Coming to, I realized my mouth was wide open, and that apparently looked like I was trying to catch flies (according to one of the girls with Sara). I quickly closed my mouth. "Yeah, sure. Let's go." Trying way too hard to sound cool and casual. My newfound friends and I headed to the store during study hall, but their praised reactions felt like an oxymoron. Their heads snapped back and forth toward each other in the backseat as they whispered to one another. Subtle snickers sounded as their bodies moved to the sound of 2000's hits filling the car.

Just like that, my "it" girl status went from a daydream to reality, and I didn't care if it was for who I was or for what I had to offer. In this case, it was my car and the freedom it symbolized during study halls, lunch breaks, and, on occasion, skipping class. I became their go-to girl for trips to the mall, to get cigarettes, and for a good time. In a twisted way, it felt amazing to be in their circle.

My chauffeur status lasted for the rest of the school year and summer. After that, one by one, each girl got her license and brand new car. And, yup, you guessed it, suddenly my worth depreciated. My car was no longer a factor, since they had the newest car on the market. That following year, I was tired of fighting to solidify my place in their circle, so I decided the shy, quirky girl I had been wouldn't work any longer and should be hidden away for good.

In her place, I morphed into someone intimidating. I suppressed my laughter, put on a tough façade, and acted out. I told myself the world did this to me, but deep down, I knew the culprit was staring back at me in the mirror.

Summertime in Vermont was filled with chilling at the lake, walking around town, and probably doing things we likely shouldn't have been doing. One day, my life shifted from being a nobody to being seen. My friend and I were walking over the Grand Union Bridge in Newport, heading back to my house after an afternoon at the skatepark. (No, I'm not a skater, but that was one of our hangout spots.) I had on silver, shimmery flare jeans that caught the sunlight like a disco ball at a rave, paired with a yellow top that read "Angel." *Oh, the irony.* Let me tell you, angelic was the last word anyone would use to describe me at that point in my life. With my fiery spirit and appetite for mischief, I was more of a fallen angel, if anything. Beside me was Ashley, who we all referred to as "Mini," mainly because she was tiny, but she had enough personality to match anyone twice her size. She was wearing her signature Adidas wind pants and t-shirt.

"Hey!" a man's voice called and was just as easily ignored. The first time I heard it, it was like a whisper compared to the noise of the bustling city around us, and I had places to be and hearts to break, after all (*mostly my own*). So, I kept walking, the sneakers under my fabulous flare jeans clunked against the worn bridge planks in a casual *swoosh-clap* rhythm. But then it came again. "HEY!" The voice was bolder, louder, and decidedly urgent this time. Mini and I exchanged glances, both wondering if we were the targets of a random catcall. We slowly turned, and the suspense felt like a small balloon inflating in my chest. I wasn't prepared for what—or rather, *who*—I'd find.

Standing there, leaning against the faded rails of the bridge, was Dan Carpenter. He was the McDreamy of my real life, and to say he was the hottest guy in town would be like calling the sun kind of warm. He had that kind of face that could stop you in your tracks and eyes you could get lost in for days.

Now, hear me when I say this bridge was hardly the romantic backdrop you'd find in novels. No ornate fixtures, no delicate designs—just weather-beaten planks beneath our feet and a view of Lake Memphremagog stretching out beneath the sky and green trees. It was, however, the seemingly unremarkable place that laid the foundation for an extraordinary love story.

My eyes darted behind me, half-expecting to find a crowd or some blonde bombshell he was actually yelling at. You know, one of those cringe-worthy moments where you wave back at someone who's waving at, *well*, not you. But there was no one else. Just me, Mini, and the wild reality that Dan Carpenter was calling to us.

My throat tightened as if I'd swallowed a whole lemon, pits and all. I turned back to face him, feeling as if I was about to step off a cliff or dive into the deep end of the pool without a life vest. As we made eye contact, something in the universe shifted, like the slight realignment of stars that occurs over centuries, except this took a matter of seconds.

When I realized he was walking toward me, my whole body blushed in a symphony of reds and pinks, as if I were a human mood ring displaying 'Embarrassed" or "Incredibly Flustered." *Why now? I've been practically invisible to him until this moment.*

Bam! We were eye to eye, soul to soul. It was like a scene out of a romantic movie where time slows down, except nobody was holding a boombox over their head or dancing in the rain. He had a friend, Nick, tagging along—a lanky guy with a grin that suggested he knew some cosmic joke we didn't. *Perfect.* Mini and Nick, the best wing people one could hope for in a moment this intense.

Dan was a smooth talker with a chiseled jawline that could probably cut glass and those eyes. Oh my GOD, those eyes— a swirling mix of gray, blue, and green that made the Caribbean Sea look like a murky pond. They pierced right through me, as if he could see that I was already falling head over heels for him.

"You ladies free later?" The words slipped out of his mouth like honey.

"We might be," Mini replied, throwing me a look that said, *Girl, if you say no, I'll kill you.*

"Great," he grinned. "How about we all meet up at Strawberry Acres? Around 5:00 p.m."

The deal was sealed, and our fates were intertwined.

Later that evening, the four of us met at Strawberry Acres, a local hotspot famous for nothing except perhaps being the place where bored teenagers went to make bad decisions. And sure, we may have been among those misguided youth, doing things we definitely shouldn't have been doing, but for some reason, that day, those ill-advised youthful escapades felt like magic spells in a fairytale.

We talked and laughed as the sky turned from shades of bright blue to deep indigo. The world around us seemed to fade away, leaving just the four of us in a bubble of happiness and, maybe, a bit of recklessness. Mini and Nick hit it off too, cackling away like two mischievous elves plotting to rig Santa's sleigh.

What struck me was how natural it felt to be with Dan. How every word we exchanged seemed to pull us closer, like two magnets coming into their inevitable alignment. How each moment spent in his presence seemed to heal a little part of me. It was enchanting and terrifying, like skydiving into an endless sky—both an exhilarating rush and a peaceful serenity.

What I didn't realize then was the monumental significance of that day. A seemingly ordinary rendezvous, filled with the careless joy of our youth, was actually the seed of something much bigger. Something lifelong. I had found my soulmate, my twin flame, and my world in a man who yelled "hey" across a bridge and turned an ordinary day into a magical moment. My heart felt like it was floating, and my stomach was filled with butterflies. I couldn't remember another time I was that at peace and had that sense of security. He didn't know it then, but he became my feeling of home. The way his warmth immediately calmed my entire being and his words kept me secure was an experience I'd never had before. This felt like love.

We were out until eleven that night. In my household, that was the equivalent of a feral teenager dancing naked around a bonfire while chanting magic spells. So, when we pulled into the VFW parking lot, the local go-to drop-off point for forbidden teenage activities, I felt the gravity of my impending doom. Mini and I had to walk with purpose on our way home, like two spies on a mission to avoid the "Mom-detection."

Mini looked at me as if she were about to deploy behind enemy lines. "Ready?"

"As I'll ever be," I whispered dramatically with a long exhale and eyeroll.

As we slinked toward my house, each step felt like I was walking deeper into the lion's den. My heart was racing, not from the magical evening but from the anxiety of the anticipated maternal eruption.

And erupt she did. The moment I set foot in the house, an explosion of anger filled the air. There were yells, there were screams, and yes, I'm pretty sure a shoe went airborne, attempting to make contact like a misguided missile.

But here's the kicker: outside the external chaos, internally, I was as calm as a monk in deep meditation. There was a serenity in knowing that I had found something—someone—worth all this drama. Dodging airborne shoes and rhetorical bullets, I felt like Neo from *The Matrix*. If Neo were a love-struck teenager grounded for the rest of her life, that is.

Finally, the sentencing came. "You're grounded for the whole summer, Alexis!" she declared, with her boyfriend chiming in as if he were the judge hammering down the gavel.

Grounded for the summer? I smirked inwardly. *Oh, buddy, you have no idea.* He wasn't even officially part of the family judiciary yet. *Who did he think he was? Judge Judy? Or should I say Judge Joe Brown?*

But you know what? I didn't care. The way I saw it, Dan was my light at the end of a very strict, flying-shoe-filled tunnel. My ray of hope in a sea of adolescent turmoil. And as for being grounded—well, let's just say it gave me plenty of time to daydream about more bridge-crossings and eye-piercing, soul-touching adventures to come.

So there I was, grounded but soaring, confined yet free, in trouble but oh-so-happily in love. If this was the price for finding my soulmate, then bring on the house arrest because that boy was worth every grounded day of summer and then some.

Chapter 13

This Is The End Of Us

The world is a vast expanse of possibilities and tragedies intermingled into a confusing existence when you're seventeen. At least, that's how it felt for me. I had been in a very complicated entanglement with Dan for what felt like forever, and he was my constant—unreliable but constant. He'd pop into my life on a random impulse, dousing me in affection for a few hours before vanishing again. He always promised to call, but the phone never rang. Consistent only in his inability to show up, keep his word, and just be what he said he was or would be.

After so long playing the cat and mouse game, I learned Dan was only coming around when it was convenient for him. I was the one to soothe his soul when no one else was there, so our sporadic situationship was a consequence of my naivety and love. I would see him twice in a month, and then six months before he came around again. I felt insignificant and betrayed. *But do I have a right to feel that way? Can't I just be happy that I have love at all?*

Instead, I carried the shame of loving a man who didn't come around when he was supposed to. I made excuses to hold onto my dignity "because he needed me." That was the issue, though: when he wasn't welcomed anywhere else, I was only good enough in a time of need. I was great at being what everyone needed when they needed it, then felt insignificant the rest of the time.

The last time he came to visit, I was ready. I had my armor on, built up from layers of disappointment and heartbreak. "Dan," I said, the weariness choking my voice. "I can't do this anymore. I'm tired of waiting around for you, like a prize you can claim when it suits you."

"Oh, yeah?" He looked me straight in the eyes—a mix of arrogance and indifference. "What if I asked you to marry me right now?"

A bitter laugh escaped my lips. "I'd say no," I retorted, meeting his gaze unwaveringly. "Nothing would change. In fact, tonight is the grand finale. We can spend it however you want—eating Wheat Thins with Cheez Whiz, drinking Coca-Cola, and smoking Marlboro full flavors. We can make love one last time, and then you will leave, and this chapter will be closed."

He laughed. He thought I was bluffing. But the fire in my eyes told a different story. It was a fierce realization of my strength even then, a resolution made after years of neglect.

That night, we did everything I said we would, and as we lay there, wrapped in each other and the bittersweet knowledge of a final goodbye, my heart ached. I embraced him tighter than ever, memorizing the scent of him and the feel of his arms around me. The morning sun filtered through the curtains, casting soft rays of light that danced on our entangled limbs. I looked into his eyes, and our lips met in a kiss that said a thousand unutterable things.

It was a kiss that said, "I'll love you forever, but you were never really mine to keep."

He left that day, just like countless times before. But this time was different. I felt the finality of it—the heavy realization that I had just let go of the only person I'd ever fully given myself to. I closed the door behind him, my hands trembling as I slid to the floor. Sobs from both loss and liberation wracked my body. The act of walking away from him was both a dagger in my heart and a reclaiming of it.

I had taken the first step in a journey to find myself, away from the chaos that was Dan. It was a step into an uncertain future, but at least it was mine. And for the first time in a long time, that felt like enough.

Shortly after saying goodbye to Dan, the last thing I imagined was that I'd fall into another's arms so quickly. But life has a strange way of presenting us with choices, some of which we make in defiance, some out of desperation, and others simply to fill a void.

I was sad after Dan and I officially walked away, determined that I would never see him again, not allowing him to come and go as he pleased.

It was a warm summer day, and I was in shorts and a tank top, feeling pretty confident in the decision I made, stronger after saying, "No more!" The problem with fake strength and motivation is that we expose ourselves to the demons that surround us, and that's exactly what happened.

I was caught off guard by the devil himself, disguised as a playful distraction. I thought it was a sign from God, but what a naïve girl I was. If only I had known it was a disguise from the devil, I would have stopped. At that time in my life, I had outward confidence like no other, but internally, I was feeling ripped apart, shameful, and unable to get anyone to love me. But if you were on the outside looking in, you would've never known because I walked around with so much sass.

This mysterious man stopped on Second Street in his black Cadillac, pulling up beside me. He rolled down his window and just tipped his sunglasses down his nose while peering at me over top of them. I smirked, swayed my hips a little bit more, and kept walking, not allowing his interest to affect me. So, instead, I carried my head high and swayed with confidence. Naturally, he chased me down. I stopped, but I was not impressed by the desperate nature of his attempt.

"Where are you going, girl?" he asked. I let out a flirtatious laugh. Snapping around just enough to give a little attitude, I said, "Wouldn't you like to know?"

It was the dangerous look in his eyes that had warning bells sounding off. Something told me I should probably stay away. Nothing good will come from this, but my broken heart and my I-don't-give-a-shit attitude wouldn't allow me to acknowledge the signs. Later that night, he was walking down my street, and when he saw me, he called me over. So, I went on the walk with him—David, that is.

It's interesting how you can fall into character based on survival tactics you learn throughout life. Like, if you want attention and anyone to choose you, you have to flirt, be desirable, and cute when they make a joke, laugh at everything, and then give a little attitude and talk back; that would drive them nuts. And I was at a point where if somebody was going to get something from me, I decided it was gonna be because I said they could have it, not simply because they took it. I was tired of feeling weak, and I was tired of going through the motions of reliving the past where people would take from me when they saw fit.

People were always taking my innocence, my childhood, and the way I should have looked at myself. I would stand in front of the mirror, repeating the hate they'd spew matching exactly how I felt about myself. Until eventually, I just stopped looking in the mirror.

A couple weeks later, I heard a ticking noise on my window. Getting up angrily, I looked out to see David throwing pebbles at my window. *Why the hell is he waking me up right now? It is nine in the morning.* I rolled my eyes.

"What do you want? It's early as hell; go away!"

"Get dressed," he interrupted. "And get down here!" The demanding tone of his voice was flirtatious and fun, so I got dressed, brushed my teeth, threw my hair up, and headed outside. I rolled my eyes again for effect and crossed my arms over my body. I have to say, it felt good to be in control. I was creating a character and decided to be whoever I wanted, and the girl I chose to be was a confident badass who nobody could fuck with, and honestly, nobody did. For a while.

At this point in my life, I had been through everything and felt life couldn't possibly get worse than it had already been for the first seventeen and a half years of my existence. So, I entertained the idea of playing and being the girl he wanted me to be. My alter ego Lexie was in control, and she was nobody to mess with. She was a sassy badass who didn't mind playing hard, doing things out of the ordinary, trying whatever came to mind, and living for the adventure. Most people didn't want to do that, but I did. I wanted any alternative reality to the one I had been living. I decided this was going to be a year of freedom to do what I wanted. Nothing serious. Except things spun out of control and went differently than I planned. Life became serious.

We started hanging out every day, and then my confidence and no-bullshit attitude began to fade. I fell in line with his commands. Suddenly, he decided it was my fault if another guy would look at me—and I would pay for it. I allowed this to be my reality, and I got burned. I was so convicted about keeping Dan at bay that I was blindsided by the monster who got too close.

Weeks passed, and Dan's attempts to reconcile became infrequent. I remained strong in my decision to leave that chapter behind, especially as my new relationship was evolving in unexpected ways. In my head, every moment I spent with David felt like a shield against Dan—a way of showing him that I was moving on. But I knew in my heart that the only reason I was dancing with the devil was because I didn't have the strength to stay away from Dan without him. Dan was my kryptonite, and I was not Superman.

One evening, as the sun was setting, David and I crossed a line we'd been tiptoeing around for four months. It felt thrilling in the moment—a heady mixture of attraction and defiance. But that thrill would soon turn to unease. As the days rolled on, David's charm began to morph into something more sinister. His words, once sweet and subtle, began to weave webs of deceit around me. He was a master manipulator, knowing exactly what to say to keep me close and to make me doubt my feelings and my decisions. His narcissism became evident in the way he constantly turned our conversations towards himself, diminishing my experiences and feelings.

I started to feel trapped, but the realization came slowly. David's manipulations were wrapped in layers of feigned affection and concern. I began to question myself, my memories, and my perceptions. It felt like being under a spell—a dark, inescapable enchantment that sapped my energy and self-worth. In my pursuit to hurt Dan and assert my independence, I had unwittingly chained myself to a toxic relationship.

Chapter 14

I'm Exposing Your Secret

WHILE DEALING with being trapped in a relationship with a narcissist, I was simultaneously navigating another form of manipulation from a "family friend," whom I would later discover was grooming me for what could have been a fatal future.

I recently watched a video clip of Taylor Swift on stage in August 2018, telling her audience that a year prior to that exact day, she was sitting in a courtroom for a sexual assault case, and the jury decided they believed her and the allegations against her assaulter. She continued to say how grateful she was for their decision, but she was also thinking about all the people who weren't believed or were too scared to say anything.

I am the woman she's referring to. And the system failed to protect me one too many times, creating a belief that had me convinced, no matter what I said, there would always be excuses as to why it happened and why what I said wasn't true. My word against theirs. And let's face it, a black woman in a family of poverty was no match for the likeness or reputation of a white man, so their word always trumped mine. I'd seen this play out in many scenarios throughout my life. This particular situation I experienced was kept a secret for twenty years out of shame, disgust, and fear, but I refuse to keep his secret anymore.

I was seventeen and naïve, so it wasn't hard to influence me as someone who just wanted to fit in and help people. When a narcissist hidden in plain sight had the trust of my mom and brother, I thought he would look out for me. Only time would quickly tell that the only intention Harley had was to manipulate a young girl, like he had so many others. Harley wasn't just an ordinary man; he was a thirty-five-year-old man incarcerated for grooming a young girl in the past.

I knew from the inappropriate nature of our conversations that he was capable of bad things. But the people I trusted believed he was a good person, so I figured I was reading it wrong. The power of narcissism is strong and can really blur the lines between the illusion of what you see and what you think you're experiencing.

Naturally, when he called my house, collect, from prison, I answered. Seeing no harm in a phone call, I carried on a normal conversation.

"Lex, I need you to do me a favor."

"Yeah, what's up?" I felt nonchalant, like it was something simple to fulfill. He asked me to go see his friend, Lee, in Windsor, Vermont, to pick up a pair of shoes and bring them to the jail for him since his mom couldn't do it.

"Sure, no problem, Harley." I collected his friend's phone number.

You know, thinking back on the situation, I realize how stupid it was. Yeah, that's how I feel sitting here now, seeing all the red flags, but I was a clueless teenager, not accustomed to the red flags of a narcissist.

I asked my mom to come to Windsor with me. I figured since my Aunt Bev lived down there, we'd just make a day of it. She agreed, and we headed south to Aunt Bev's. When we got there after our hour-and-a-half drive, I called Lee to let him know where I was. He showed up around twenty minutes later, and I asked where the shoes were.

"Oh, I just got done with work, so I figured I'd pick you up and we could grab a bite to eat as a thank you for driving all this way."

I looked to my mom and aunt for direction, and they just shrugged. "Save me some chocolate chip cookies," I told them. "I'll be back soon." I hopped into his little two-door red car. He asked me a lot of questions, which kept the conversation flowing as I answered him. About fifteen minutes later, we got to his house, and I realized I left my purse and phone at my aunt's. My stomach did a little flip at the realization, but I ignored it as he directed me into his home.

"They're in the bedroom. Follow me; I'll give you a tour of the place," he said without missing a beat.

"Is your wife home? How old are you?" My questions spilled out faster than intended. My eyes widened as I realized the speed at which his full body turned. It was so immediate that I bumped into him. Stepping back, I said, "Oh my God, I'm so sorry! Are you okay?"

There was something in his eyes when he replied, "Fine. No wife. Forty-one." One word for each answer, and my whole body stiffened. Scenarios started running through my mind, and I began to realize I didn't have my phone, my car, my purse, his address—nothing. I didn't stop to think and ask for his address to give to my mom and aunt. I just so trustingly got in the car, told my mom I'd be back soon, and left.

He turned back around. "This is the kitchen. The bathroom's over to the right, and here's my bedroom. Follow me." There was an authoritative tone to his voice that caused me to jump, but I obeyed. His room was small with little room to maneuver around, so I stood in the doorway, but he asked for my help as they were under his bed on the side furthest from the door. He told me he couldn't reach them and needed my help grabbing them from under the bed. Heart racing, I slowly walked over to the enclosed side of the bed, and he pointed in front of where he was standing. My eyes followed his stubby finger. Suddenly, I felt vulnerable and exposed in my shorts, tank top, and sandals.

"The box is a good length under there, so you'll probably have to get down there."

A nervous laugh escaped my mouth, and he smiled so sadistically that I could have vomited right there. Against every instinct and the will of every fiber of my being, I did what he said. Down on my hands and knees, I peered under the bed, but I could only think about the exposed parts of my body and the sensation of his eyes burning through me as he scanned every inch of me. I could hear his breathing become labored and louder.

"You might have to get your upper body under there to see it," he doubles down. I feel around, not wanting to turn my head to face under the bed but knowing I have to in order to find the shoes quicker. So, I turn my head to face under the bed, blind to the rest of the room.

I jumped at the feeling of Lee's hand on the back of my thigh, and another nervous sound came out of my mouth involuntarily. He tightened his grip on the back of my leg, and I pushed out from underneath the bed.

"I'm not here for that, Lee. I just came for the shoes."

He hovered over me. His tongue darts out of his mouth to lick his lips. I was at a disadvantage, being on the floor to look under the bed. He grabbed my arm and pulled me upward, and I relaxed, thinking he got the hint and was simply helping me up. Upright again, my back was to the wall and he blocked my only way out of the room. *Unless I can get across the bed.* I hesitated, but then tried to leap as far as I could across the bed, but he grabbed me.

"Oh, you want to play, my beautiful girl? Good, because I want to play. I'm going to do things that'll make you feel really good."

I shake my head no. "No. That's not what I came here for." A small cry escaped my lips, only making him more eager.

He gripped me tighter around the legs, and his scratchy fingers moved around my body as I screamed, "No! Please stop." Each time quieter than the last. My head tilted upward and away from him, and my hands splayed on his chest, attempting to push him away. He managed to climb his way on top of me, and I left my body. I was lifeless, staring down from above, telling myself, *We just need to survive. If you fight, he might kill you or keep you here, and no one knows where you are or who he is.* Everything went black. I was numb. I wanted to die. I wanted to run. I wanted to scream. But I did nothing. I laid there numb, wishing for it to be over.

I don't know how long it was, but it felt like forever. I quickly covered myself when I realized he got off me and left the room in nothing but his white underwear. I tried to recall when he had removed all his clothes, confused. The whole experience had trapped me in my mind, a mind that kept playing the same loop: *No one will ever believe you.* I was stuck in my own mental cage, unable to break free from the monstrous memories claiming my body.

Bile rose in my throat, my veins filled with creeping terror. I kept drifting in and out of reality, into a dissociative state where my physical body became numb, lost in a sea of darkness. Yet, I had to strategize my escape, or lack thereof, from this nightmarish reality that I had walked into so unsuspectingly.

He twisted my innocent intention of doing a favor into a violation of my body and spirit. Oh, God, he took advantage of me; my voice was a mere whisper, barely audible even to my own ears: *I said, no, please no. I don't want this. I said, oh, God, who will believe me? He didn't listen.* The helplessness of these thoughts was overwhelming.

The betrayal was not just in the act itself but also in the shame and stigma that followed. It's like society has its own script for survivors, and I couldn't escape the suffocating weight of blame and guilt that lay upon my shoulders.

Old voices echoed in my mind, firing off accusations like shots from a gun. "You asked for it," they'd say. "You're a whore," "This is all your fault," "You're dirty, damaged goods that no one will ever love." I couldn't turn off the noise. It felt like I was drowning in a sea of blame, gasping for breath but only inhaling a cruel mix of shame and guilt.

Minutes dragged on like agonizing years. When he was finished, his deafening words hit my chest like a ton of bricks. He asked what movie I wanted to watch, as if we were just friends hanging out, completely oblivious to the personal nightmare he'd put me through. He even mentioned making stuffed chicken breasts, shooting a lustful glance at my chest that made my skin crawl. Maybe I nodded; his words were a meaningless buzz in my ears. I was struck by the grim reality: I had to continue sitting there, engaging in this awful charade, while screaming internally.

The shoes. That was why I went there in the first place. A ridiculous reason that seemed so important then, but now? They mean nothing. The darkness settles outside and light from the streetlamps shine through his window. I ask myself, *Why me? What did I do to deserve this? Why did the people who said they loved me allow this to happen?* In that moment, death seemed like a beautiful escape, a way out of a situation that had become terrorizing.

I was jerked back to reality when he touched my shoulder, making me regret my choice of a tank top in the 80-degree weather. My eyes flew open as his hand moved toward my chest. I felt the bile rise in my throat, paralyzed, my heart pounding like a drum. I was his prey, a hunted deer, vulnerable and terrified. I sat there for an endless number of minutes, not knowing what he would do next but desperate to leave.

The dark wood paneling on his walls caught my eye as I slowly turned to avoid eye contact. It is a wall forever seared into my memory. He broke my trance when he spoke. "Eat your dinner. You don't want to upset me after I just cooked a hot meal for you, do you? Eat up, and then we'll watch a movie before I bring you home." He said it so casually, like he didn't just rape me.

Every word was a blow, filling me with dread and despair. But I did what he said, with a determination to survive. I ate the food as quickly as I could, leaving half on the plate and claiming I couldn't eat anymore. The movie felt as if it lasted forever, as I sat there visibly trembling, counting the minutes until it was over. The ride back to Aunt Bev's felt like an eternity. Every bump in the road, every turn of the tires, was a painful reminder of the hellish ordeal I'd just been through. As I stepped out of the car, I was met by the night sky, painted in a deep, dark blue, barely illuminated by the moon and stars. It should've been beautiful, but I couldn't see it that way.

My mom and Aunt Bev were there on the porch, waiting for me, their faces lit up by the soft porch light. They asked how it went, a seemingly innocent question that felt like a knife to my gut. I couldn't answer them. Their words were drowned out by the cacophony of thoughts screaming in my head. I walked past them without a word, my eyes fixed on the ground, and headed straight for the bathroom.

I locked the door behind me, peeled off my clothes, and stepped into the shower. I turned the water on as hot as it would go, as if scalding water could wash away the dirty, stained feeling that clung to me. The water cascaded over my body, but it did nothing to cleanse the filth I felt on my skin and even less for the stains on my soul. Eventually sliding down in the bathtub, letting the water run over me until it turned ice cold.

Mindlessly scratching at my skin in a futile effort to remove the invisible marks left on me. I eventually turned the water off, not feeling cleansed; instead, it was as if the stains had seeped into my very being, marks that no amount of water or soap could ever remove. As I sat there, shivering in the cold that was now trickling from the showerhead, I realized this was a secret I'd likely carry to my grave. Because in that moment, shrouded in my own thoughts and society's judgments, I felt unworthy of belief, unworthy of... everything.

That was one of the longest nights of my life, the start of a journey no one should ever have to take. It was ultimately why I found myself leaning on liquid courage just to get through my haunted nights and anxious days. I couldn't escape the vivid memory; every touch a searing brand on my skin, every sensation a visceral reminder of that horrible night.

I am able to look at this now and have come to understand that he alone bears the blame for his actions. I was not and am not at fault for what happened. I am now learning to heal two decades later. One form of healing is redefining my boundaries. Another is to use my experience to guide me and find a way to be there for others who have endured the same darkness. This book has given me my voice, and I pray that if you're searching for yours, you learn to look within yourself to find it.

Chapter 15

In And Out Of Darkness

Burning bridge after bridge, I would often wonder when the cycle would end. *When do I meet the people meant for me?* Suffocating in my small town in Vermont, I had to get out. *Nothing good will ever come from staying here. Really, though, what good was coming from being here? Drunken nights and numbing the pain of my life over and over?*

Lying to myself, I'd often say I didn't have a problem. Looking back now, I realize how bad it really got. I worked three jobs, and the moment I'd get off my last shift, I would drink until about four or five in the morning, only to get up around six o'clock to go back to work and do it all over again. I got so good at hiding from the world; it was truly a flawless system—except I was literally killing myself. I was suffering from alcohol poisoning, the loss of friends, and myself.

I remember this one party I went to at a girlfriend's house when I was seventeen. I consumed a fifth of Jack Daniel's, two bottles of Boone's Farm, a six-pack of Smirnoff Ice, and two beers on an empty stomach and still felt like I needed more. My heart ached so badly; I wanted to numb life forever. I thought if I just drank at these parties, all my pain would go away. Usually, I'd have a small amount of alcohol to consume, but this was like a candy store. With every dark thought that entered my mind, another sip would come. Before I knew it, the thoughts increased, and the bottles seemed to go down faster and faster. My friends were telling me to slow down, that it was a lot, but I wanted it to be a lot: I wanted it to take me away from the pain forever.

The next thing I remember is being in my friend's room and blacking out. In and out, the darkness was taking me, and then I'd hear faint voices and come back to the light. Blurred figures, saying things I couldn't understand, just muffled sounds like I was submerged underwater. Eventually, I came through enough to hear, "We need to call 9-1-1." But another voice said, "We can't; my mom will get in trouble for the alcohol and underage drinking." At that moment, I knew my life wasn't more important than a reprimand. I was a liability. But there was a bigger dilemma. "What if she dies?" one of them asked.

I heard a weird one-sided conversation, and then, "Okay, bye." Followed by, "My mom said to call the ambulance and just say we took the liquor out of the cabinet when she went to work." Everyone agreed.

Things went dark again until I felt a searing pain in my chest. It was the knuckles of someone pushing extremely hard against my chest, rubbing their knuckles up and down. I cried out and then heard, "She's back!"

Sirens, lights, people. It was all so much; I had no idea what was going on. Met with the angry faces of the police, my mom, and the doctors of the ER, not able to make out all of their words nor able to form words of my own. Tubes went down in my throat as my stomach was pumped and I urinated on myself. I remember, at that very moment, pulling that chain off my neck and squeezing it. *If only God could save me this time; I won't do it again.* I was scared, no longer worried about releasing the pain in an eternal sense, but focused on surviving. Something I'd never wanted to do before.

All of a sudden, things started to go dark again. Doctors rushed around me, and my mom began to panic. I remember grabbing her hand and holding my St. Mary necklace between our hands. My hand went limp, and I went dark. I don't remember anything after that until I woke up in my room. No one was home—just me, alone with my thoughts. I tried to sit up, and the room was still spinning. I had to slide down the side of my bed like a snake sliding down a tree, and then continue crawling to the bathroom. If I didn't have vision, I would have thought my lower body was gone because of the sensation of paralysis. I inched my way to the bathroom, stopping to cry every five seconds. I finally made it to the bathroom and had to leverage the tub and sink next to me to lift up toward the toilet. Unsteadily going to the bathroom, I cried and repeated, "Oh God, why?"

At that very moment, I never wanted to feel this way again, and little did I know, the court system would make sure I wouldn't be able to touch another drink for a very long time. In Vermont, underage drinking is highly frowned upon, especially when death is nearly the end result. But I didn't realize this was only the beginning of a long journey.

This is where I was introduced to counseling. A part of my court stipulations was to attend weekly counseling, drug tests, and volunteer work at the library. My counselor was incredible, and I found a unique freedom in confiding in someone who legally couldn't tell anyone my secrets. Well, unless you told them you wanted to harm yourself, but since I already did that, our conversations centered around why I felt that way.

I told portions of the truth, but not that such terrible things had happened to me that I wanted to end my life. Not that I was manipulated by multiple people and had to hide it from the world. Not that I didn't feel worthy of living. I only told the little truths like, "I want to be loved" and "Why does everyone abandon me?" And before you knew it, at eight months into counseling, my third therapist decided I was cured. That's the exact moment I ran back to drinking the harsh amber liquid just to get through the day.

Alcohol always felt like my escape, my courage to conquer the fucked-up world. I felt nothing, so everyone else could feel something both figuratively and literally. It was nearly the death of me on more occasions than I'd like to admit.

By that time, I was the queen of showing up in a way that said, "I've got the confidence of a millionaire, even when I had nothing but a pot to piss in." I created a world of desire, lust, and attraction; only I wasn't attractive; I was performing. I hid for decades, showing up like I could have anything and everything I wanted. Men would look at me like I was a snack they couldn't wait to try, but I would allow in only those I truly desired. Unfortunately, those seemed to be the people I should have kept as far away from me as possible. I continued to trap myself in relationships that were like cancer, sucking the soul out of me one cell at a time.

Chapter 16

Little Red Rabbit Foot

Have you ever had a place that felt like your escape, where you're surrounded by trust and safety? Being with Aunt Jen and Uncle John was that sanctuary for me. I would go to them during any crisis, and they would love me through it. They always lovingly gave me advice when I sought it and shared their opinions, but they never forced me to take it. They helped me see a different perspective, rather than only the judgment of my actions or the situation I might've been in.

After I almost died from alcohol poisoning when I was seventeen, I visited Aunt Jen and Uncle John in Burlington. Although they were disappointed in my actions which almost caused me to leave them earthside, they were always far more concerned with my well-being. They made sure I knew I belonged, just how loved I was, and the devastation my absence would have caused. My uncle told me how scared they were and how incredibly important it was that I took all of my life into consideration, not just the ugly moments but the good, the bad, and beyond. At any moment, everything could change, and that's the beauty of living.

Sometimes we hurt, and it's easy to find that quick solution—to just walk away and be done with the pain. But when we realize we can never fully move through the pain until we understand how to sit with it and feel what we're feeling, that's when we become unstoppable.

Uncle John had a red rabbit foot in his hands; it was supposed to be a symbol of good luck and protection. He said, handing it to me, "When things start to get dark, hold onto it, and let it be your reminder of all the people who love and cherish you. We would all be so sad without you here. You have so much joy to live for."

Hold onto it; I did. Like a lifeline. That was the only thing that could ever save me. Still to this day, I have that red rabbit foot in one of my purses in my closet that I pull out every now and then and rub on its worn-out side, bare from years of rubbing it like it was a genie in a paw while thinking of where I wanted to be rather than sitting in very uncomfortable situations.

During my relationship with David, my aunt and uncle were so extremely concerned, and I remember cutting the relationship off. I was so ashamed of the things that I had done. If only I had remembered that throughout all my faults and poor choices, they were always by my side. But I was in such a state of scarcity and a negative mindset that I felt unworthy of their love. I felt so much shame for being in an abusive and toxic relationship that I didn't go to them.

They were there for me then and still are today, even in the darkest moments. I could never repay the kindness, generosity, and unconditional love that they have shown me my entire life.

I know without a doubt that I would not be the woman that I am today without them as a beacon and a guiding light.

Out of all the people I told, they were the most excited about me writing this book. When I shared my concerns about being dyslexic and reading aloud wondering if people would laugh at me, we just made jokes about it. They made it so lighthearted that none of my fears even mattered to me anymore—the only thing that mattered to them was that I pushed forward and was brave enough to share these vulnerable stories.

I want someone who is struggling to know *I've been there*. I was trying to find my place in the world and got stuck in a cycle of craving a sense of belonging. When really, I could've looked inside myself and known that I belonged to *me* all along. I was conditioned to feel that I needed other people to validate me. I needed to feel worthy of somebody else's love, no matter the circumstance or the situation. I was so attached to anyone who would show me any type of attention that I didn't understand or realize the difference between true love and affection and manipulation and narcissism.

If you don't—if you truly don't have that somebody in your life who can be a shining light to guide you, love you, and support you through your hardships—know that I am here. My inbox is always open, day and night, and I will do my best to respond to everybody who reaches out in need to share their heart and their pain.

I know that my purpose in life is to do something bigger—bigger than me, bigger than my community. This is a global impact that I'm destined to make. When I think about survival and the navigation of life, I don't think that we make wrong turns or wrong choices.

I believe that our choices are made to give us wisdom and the ability to provide guidance for those who come after us. We are all worthy of love. When we seek love in the right, most healthy way, we will never desire somebody else to validate us. But first, we have to be able to provide ourselves with the love we need.

Survival mode is a temporary solution, not a permanent resolution. Life is too short to go through it scared, feeling ashamed of who you are and what you've been through. One of the biggest obstacles is overcoming your own shame and guilt and forgiving yourself. If we can't do that, we will fail to reach out for support, love, and help. This does not make you a weak person. This makes you one of the strongest people you'll ever know.

I know because I went through it. I know that there is another path, and there is always somebody in real life who is willing to help, listen, and care. Someone to love me enough to help me through the hard moments. I'm grateful I had my aunt and uncle to call and love me through it.

Chapter 17

Dating the Devil

I went years believing I had earned a golden ticket straight to hell. I thought there was no way God loved me; I didn't love me, and no one else seemed to love me either. Well, except for my brother, but he was locked away like a caged bird. At the time, I believed he might have even hated me after finding out what I'd done. There was one thing that kept me believing that maybe there was hope for me: God kept whispering, "My dear child, I will love you forever. Tell me your sin and ask me for forgiveness, and His will shall be done."

"God, could you truly forgive me?" I'd ask this question multiple times a day. Then I'd stop and look at myself in the mirror. Upon seeing nothing but disappointment, I'd think, *Even if He did, I'd never forgive me.*

As days turned into nights, nights into weeks, and weeks into months, my life felt like it was skidding away from me, like a car out of control on icy roads. I could hear the distant voices of friends and family, their cautionary advice echoing in my ears, but their words seemed like muffled conversations compared to the loud resonance of David's manipulations.

Then I lost my apartment. Kicked out of my mom's place, David swooped in like some warped superhero, his van doubling as my new residence. For the next six months, it was his work van by day and my home at night. We lived in that van, braving a winter that plunged into subzero temperatures. We huddled under a single comforter, relying on body heat for warmth, as if that could compensate for the icy chill in our relationship.

When my birthday neared—a day that should have been about celebration—it felt like a prelude to catastrophe. With a dollar store pregnancy test clutched in my hand, I called my friend Jamie.

"Can you meet me at my mom's?" I asked, my voice tinged with desperation.

When Jamie saw the test, her eyes filled with a silent apology. I dripped the droplets of pee on the strip, and the result came back clear and unmistakable. *Pregnant.*

That night, I returned to Jamie's house—the place that once reverberated with our laughter, dancing, and toasts to youthful recklessness. This time, however, the atmosphere was different, imbued with a heaviness that could not be lifted. David sensed it immediately.

"What's going on with you?" he inquired, his eyes narrowing.

"Nothing; I'm fine," I lied. "I just don't want to drink tonight." As if on cue, my hands instinctively moved to protect my stomach.

Without another word, he poured a glass of Jack Daniel's neat—a whiskey I'd vowed to never touch again. He swung the glass toward me, spilling half its contents onto my lap.

"What the fuck? No. I'm not drinking tonight," I protested.

Ignoring me, he brought the glass to my lips, pushing past my attempts to swat his hand away. The liquid forced its way down my throat, choking me, the scent of whiskey filling my nostrils as it overflowed. I finally managed to push him away and staggered to the bathroom, where I broke down in a haze of despair and confusion.

David's angry pounding on the bathroom door finally ceased after what felt like an eternity. Stepping out, I looked at David, who locked eyes with me and said, "You're getting rid of it."

"Getting rid of what?" I feigned ignorance, but before I could react, his fist connected with my stomach. The breath whooshed out of me as I keeled over in pain, tears streaming down my face, and fear for my unborn child washed over me.

"I'm sorry, little one," I whispered, realizing the horrifying depths to which my life had sunk. If this was rock bottom, then the only way left was up. But for the first time, it wasn't just about me. There was another life to consider, and the weight of that responsibility broke me—but it also offered a glimmer of the strength I'd need.

We slept on Jamie's kitchen floor that night, a cold, unforgiving surface that seemed fitting for the circumstances. David continued to pinch my stomach, pressing down hard enough that I began to bleed. His words were absent of any empathy as he scheduled an appointment for an abortion, completely disregarding that the date coincided with my birthday. The cruel irony of it left me feeling like I was in some twisted movie

—a story written by an author who reveled in devastating their characters.

I can't stress enough how easy it is to now say, "I should have left." When you're trapped in a spiderweb of abuse and manipulation, every struggle to break free only ensnares you more. My life was a mess; I had nothing except a flicker of self-worth that was quickly becoming ash. At seventeen, what logic do you have? In my case, none.

So, I sat in the waiting room of the clinic, staring at the cold linoleum floor. A voice inside me screamed, "Leave! Get up and leave!" But my body felt like it was weighed down with lead. Just as I was mustering the last bit of courage to stand, the sound of my name broke the silence: "Alexis Simon."

Walking into that room was like walking into a nightmare I couldn't wake up from. Happy murals adorned the ceiling, a gross contrast to the clinical machinery surrounding me. As the staff listed off the procedures and paperwork, one line stood out: my insurance wouldn't cover anesthesia; Tylenol would be my only relief.

Minutes felt like seconds. Before I knew it, a white tube labeled "vacuum" was presented. The pain that followed was unbearable—a physical torment that felt like a punishment. *I deserve this pain*, I told myself. *I'm deserving of every excruciating moment.* My heart wasn't just breaking; it was being pulverized into a billion shards. I prayed, I cried, and I screamed silently, begging for it all to stop. But they didn't stop until they were finished. My baby was gone; it vanished like a brief flicker of light in a vast darkness. And the worst part? I was the reason. My paralyzing fear had overridden any protective instincts I might have had.

I died that day.

Not in a physical sense, but the person I was—the person who still had hope that things would be alright—was extinguished. The choices I had made, or let be made for me, became my straitjacket, a shame that sunk its teeth deep into my soul. My healing wasn't just a matter of stitching up wounds; it was about finding a way to breathe life into a part of me that felt irrevocably lost.

That night was another instance of my body being reduced to nothing more than an object, a thing he felt he had the right to control.

"I can't tonight, David. Because of the procedure," I tried to explain, but my words were nothing more than air dissipating in the wind as he covered my mouth and did to me what he desired. The hormones, the emotional and physical pain—they all made me feel as if my will to live was hanging by the thinnest of threads. I hated him. My body was his playground, his object of twisted affection, something for him to do with as he pleased.

As he carried on, I was getting really good at leaving the room mentally, allowing my consciousness to drift to another place. Detachment became my temporary savior. Alcohol became my closest companion again; I needed to be drunk all the time to make the incessant pain bearable. The numbness it brought was a desperate form of relief. I would drink until the world was a blurry, incomprehensible mess, until my body felt distant, like an object that moved me from point A to point B —no more than a vessel to be exploited, without a soul to feel the degradation.

Life took an ironic turn a few months later. I was pregnant again, an inception likely dating back to that very day when my first child's life, and a part of mine, had been extinguished. *But this time would be different*, I told myself. How it would be different, I wasn't sure. I was attending school in Chicopee, Massachusetts, living on a shoestring budget and under the looming threat from my mother that if I ever got pregnant, I would be on my own.

So, there I was, standing at the payphone in my dorm like every other day, praying for his call. It was a routine that left me skipping meals as I waited with bated breath to pick up on the first ring. Then came a day when one of the girls in the dorm had had enough of my hogging the phone. She parked herself in front of the payphone, monopolizing it for what felt like hours. I couldn't tell if she was even talking to anyone, but she seemed intent on making a point.

My heart raced with every passing minute; anxiety enveloped me like a shroud. The phone was my umbilical cord to a grim reality, and she was severing it without knowing the layers of my desperation. Here I was, carrying another life within me, still attached to a man who had crushed me in every way possible. I felt cornered, but it was in that very moment of despair that something within me began to stir a newfound determination to protect the life inside me and salvage what was left of my own.

I remember every detail of that day. I headed toward the front office because it was evident the girl in my dorm had no plans of leaving the phone. I needed a phone, and fast. That's when I heard David's voice behind me on campus, and my body went into a state of paralysis. Slowly turning around, I was already calculating what I would say to placate him. The air between us was thick with tension, almost electric.

"Go to the car now," he commanded.

I rushed to his sleek black Cadillac, its dark-tinted windows concealing whatever was inside. Once in, I attempted small talk, nervous laughter filling the uncomfortable silence. He started driving.

"Where were you?" he snapped, cutting through my chatter. "Someone said they hadn't seen you all day."

"I was waiting by the payphone, just like you told me to," I stammered. The car filled with a silence so profound that it seemed to vibrate through my bones.

"Cut the shit," he seethed. The car swerved abruptly as he took an exit. Panicked, I pushed his hand back toward the highway. He slammed the car onto the shoulder, his eyes aflame. Before I knew it, his fists were pounding into my chest, each hitting a punctuation mark in his rage. "Get out of the fucking car!" He threw open the passenger door, and I hesitated until he screamed it again. "Get the fuck out!"

He slammed his fist into my chest with each word. I jumped out, barely able to close the door before he sped off, leaving me stranded on the side of the highway.

As I walked to the nearest gas station to use a payphone, I thought about my life and what I had allowed it to come to. Luckily, I had the number of my school memorized, so I asked my resident assistant, Mr. Brown, if he could come get me. Shortly after, Mr. Brown pulled up. His face was a mixture of concern and fury.

"What the hell happened? Someone who's supposed to protect you shouldn't leave you like this. You could've been killed."

His words struck a chord deep within me. For the first time, I realized how badly I needed to protect myself, not just for my sake but for the life inside me.

"I'm not mad at you," my RA continued. "But you need to figure this shit out before you end up missing, or worse, dead."

The ride back was a sobering reflection. I stared out of the window, haunted by the day's events. The realization that I was a pawn in a sick game began to dawn on me. As much as I felt like a victim, I also felt a new sense of responsibility.

That day, I sat in Mrs. Renner's office, letting my tears flow freely. I had made up my mind; I was going to have this baby and leave David and all the chains that bound me to him. I could do this, despite my mother's heartless words that echoed in my mind. *If you're pregnant, don't even bother coming home; I want nothing to do with it or you. I don't plan to raise more kids; I already raised you.* I didn't know how she knew, but the knowledge that she wouldn't be there for me made it harder and created more uncertainty in my vision of life after school. Another girl on campus was pregnant, and she had her partner beside her—a picture of what could be, except I knew that picture would never be mine.

My resolve was strong, but the next day, David showed up at my school, carrying Chinese food as if he could fix things with a simple meal. Mr. Brown looked out the window, wearing an expression that screamed, "This is a bad idea." I gave him a half-smile, as if to say, "Don't worry, I've got this." *But did I?*

I listened to David's apologies and, against my better judgment, got into the car. He took me to his parents' house, where I was confined to the basement like some shameful secret, even being made to go to the bathroom outdoors. Kidnapped, I told him about my decision to keep the baby and offered him an out: he could leave if he didn't want to be part of this. His answer? A violent tirade that left me bruised, both physically and emotionally. He stole my car keys when I wasn't looking, and as if that wasn't enough, he made it clear I was going to be a single mother to a "bastard child," just like me.

The horror unfolded again; he tripped me down the stairs, forced alcohol down my throat, and left me alone in the dark, cold basement. The next morning, he drove me to a clinic in Springfield, Massachusetts, with an ultimatum. "Bring back the paperwork to prove you've gone through with it or else. I'm not fucking kidding with you, Alexis."

So there I was, in another cold room, my body trembling, heartbroken again. David had my keys, my only way out, and he would hold them hostage until I showed proof. February 7, 2007 marked the day the world saw me break wide open. There was no putting me back together, not this time.

But something inside me also hardened that day. I made a vow to myself: I would walk away from this horror, from him, and I would never look back. Even if it did take me another grueling year-and-a-half to finally break free, I did it. And this time it was for good. I was free from the monster, but not from shame.

Moving back to my mom's house was like a time warp; everything was the same but different. I felt like a faded photograph, out of place among the vivid colors of life that flowed around me. I found a job at the local convenience store, Cumbie's, that didn't demand much of me, and it suited the nothingness I felt inside.

Weekends saw me traveling down to Connecticut, checking into run-down hotels, just to lose myself in bottles of oblivion. I didn't care. My body was a hollow shell, and I allowed it to be treated as such. I drank till I was numb, woke up, and did it all over again. There was no "me" to protect anymore, no dreams to aspire to, just an endless loop of self-destructive behavior.

But then, one day, a small flicker of self-respect sparked within me when I called David, and his girlfriend, Amber, answered. *Yup*, girlfriend. The girl he was dating three and a half years prior who was supposed to no longer be in the picture. It was a faint flicker, but it was there. I decided to take my job seriously. It may have been a simple job at a convenience store, but it was a job, and it was mine. For six solid months, I didn't call out sick once. I took on extra shifts, filling in for others and doing better, pushing myself to excel in a job that nobody expected much from.

With each passing day, I felt a tiny piece of myself returning. The numbness began to recede, making way for glimmers of self-worth, self-respect, and eventually, self-love. It was a long and treacherous journey, but I stuck to it because, at that point, what other choice did I have? My world had already fallen apart; the only direction I could go was up.

That seemingly insignificant job became my steppingstone— my therapy. Every shift I covered, every extra hour I put in, added another stitch to the gaping wounds in my soul. I wasn't whole yet, not by a long shot, but I was less broken than before, and sometimes that's all you can ask for. This was the turning point in my life. I knew I'd never let anyone dictate my decisions, my voice, or my heart.

Chapter 18

Performance Of A Lifetime

I was born into addiction, both figuratively and literally. Now, before your brain turns to judgment, I caution you to pause. At every point in our lives, we are doing the very best we can at any given moment. We only know what we know, and we only go as far as we're willing to grow. I understand growth is a big thing nowadays, but my parents didn't really have exposure to that mindset and lifestyle. They were raised with the philosophy, "You get what you get and make do."

I followed the route the system had created for a girl like me. For a while, I was living proof of it. But then I realized I didn't have to be or do anything I chose not to be. Unfortunately, I needed more than just awareness of that fact to make a real change. My behavior kept me in the same cycle because, again, we only know what we know. So, my days often sounded like this.

Beep. Beep. Beep.

The invasive sound that blared pierced through my peaceful sleep, and my hand flailed wildly in an effort to make it stop. Upon finding nothing but air instead of the alarm's snooze button, I'd pry one eye open and glance around, realizing the noise wasn't coming from my bedside table but buried beneath my crumpled clothes from last night.

That familiar scent of old rum wafted up to greet me as I'd groggily unravel myself from the sheets, staggering toward the pile. Memories of last night played in my hungover mind. Laughter, shots, and sloppy goodbyes. An all-too-familiar routine.

"Ugh!" My groans were a protest, and they always seemed to get louder with each step as I would unsteadily walk the short distance to silence the persistent alarm. Finally finding it and flicking it off with an over-exaggerated eye roll, as if it would actually faze the phone.

My life, you might say, was pretty routine. I got hammered, stumbled back home alone, dropped my drawers to the floor, and dove into bed. Or sometimes I'd quite literally be diving to the floor because my depth perception was so far off that I'd miss the bed by a mile. The consequence? A trace of evidence of the festivities from the night before was my bruised chocolaty caramel skin, which often went unnoticed by the oblivious eye.

Then, it was like I would go into soulless auto-pilot; I'd proceed through the motions of the day. Before fully waking, I'd find myself at job number one: Troy General Store. On my second cup of bitter coffee, my eyelids would still be heavy from exhaustion, but surrender was not an option. I felt sorry for myself every chance I got, using it as an excuse to make bullshit choices that landed me nowhere but in bad positions and one decision away from disaster.

Another four a.m. bedtime with the girls, a lonely hour of rest, and I'd be back, cycling through my trifecta of dead-end jobs. A quick meet-up with my bestie Charlene, and we were off to Griff's Pub. After that, it'd be a blur of shots of Captain Morgan—no chasers because I felt too cool for that. Especially with everyone's eyes of envy on me, validating that feeling. They'd say, "Oh my God, you're such a badass. I can't believe you drink that without a chaser and don't even flinch." My response was often a sly smile and a phrase like, "There's no other way to do it. I love the burn. Let's do another one!" I'd repeat this in between the tall glasses of Captain and Coke until everything went dark, blissfully void of any emotion.

Most of the time, I couldn't recall how I'd miraculously made it home. But every time I would manage to find my way back, I'd shed clothes, items, and all my consciousness in one clumsy, intoxicated dance before collapsing into bed just like every night before. A few brief hours later, the alarm sounded, initiating the endless cycle once more.

There's got to be more to life than this... It was an unconscious whisper—or maybe a plea—as I moved through each day, surrounded by people yet enveloped in hidden loneliness. No answer ever came, no divine intervention, no profound epiphany —just the echo of my own thoughts in the silent emptiness.

I felt like life taunted me every chance it got. A bullshit repetitive mockery of existence, lacking purpose, devoid of real connection. The moments of inebriated joy with the girls were brief, and the laughter was momentary, dissipating like mist in the harsh light of reality each morning. Sometimes I'd wonder why I kept doing this to myself. Maybe, in those brief instances of what I thought was blissful unawareness, I could escape the relentless haunting question: *Is this all there is?*

But this persistent cycle of self-destruction would wrap itself around me like a comforting but toxic blanket. A familiar routine of chaos. But that whisper, that desperate, desolate whisper, never ceased perpetually nipping at the heels of my consciousness, hinting at the possibility, or maybe the fantasy, of something more. I'd held onto this feeling throughout my life but never really explored what it meant.

Some people were addicted to the sting of the needle, and others were addicted to the cold liquid moving through their veins. Others, like me, became addicted to the amber liquid running down our chest and settling into the pit of our stomach. The warm feeling was comforting, as it relieved the tension of my everyday life.

It's ironic, though; I genuinely believed I didn't have a problem. It wasn't until a random winter morning that the atmosphere seemed colder than usual. It seemed to mirror the hard truth I was faced with, staring back at myself harshly in the reflection. Twenty years old, barely an education, three dead-end jobs, no money saved—just the fleeting memories of drunken stupor. All those sleepless nights chasing away the pain with alcohol.

When one bottle was gone, I'd move onto the next, not wanting to feel. Having a high alcohol tolerance was the only goal I was striving for, training my body to be a champion of drinking. It took me a solid year and a half to build up my ability to drink seven to eight strong Captain and Cokes and upwards of ten shots a night. I was a professional at watching the room spin, eventually seeing blobs of people instead of actual figures—everyone would just melt together, and I'd be left there lost in a sea of sounds.

The day I realized I had a problem started like every other, but the pattern changed slightly when I got to my second job doing customer service at Jay Peak Resort. We were particularly busy this day, filling the demands of the season pass holders and ensuring they got their early bird pricing.

"Hi, how are you today? Are you renewing your season's pass for a single member or family pass?" The responses differed, but everyone seemed to represent the same energy: excitement for the season to begin but not fond of conversation with the girl who still smelled of alcohol from the night before.

I swear I looked at the clock a million times that day, only to find three to five minutes passing between each glance. The clock struck noon, and I went to take my break when I saw my boss coming into the office. I held the door for him when he stopped and asked how I was. I told him I was good; just going to take a break and maybe grab something to eat (even though I knew I'd use my time smoking cigarettes and drinking coffee, my typical diet).

"We've gotten some complaints about you today, and I know you probably had a night out; you're young," he gave me a half smile. "But you smell like liquor. I'm gonna have to send you home. Come back tomorrow sober, and I would recommend not smelling like alcohol." I stared blankly at him and just nodded my head as shame washed over me. I returned to the office space to retrieve my purse and keys as quickly as I could. The two girls I worked with looked at me with pity and judgment. I left without saying anything to anyone.

I spent the remainder of that day driving around, eventually returning to my apartment in Derby. I walked in to find my apartment freezing again. I quickly went to check the hot water, but the water ran cold, so I went to the heater, and aside from the creaking noise, it did nothing. I called the heating service provider, and they told me my propane ran out again, even though they were just there last week. It was going to cost me $190.00 for the emergency visit and *then* the cost of the propane, and that couldn't be less than one hundred gallons. I said, "Okay," and gave my card over the phone for the emergency fee.

When I hung up, I quickly called my bank to find out my remaining balance. "Thank you for calling Community National Bank. To hear your balance, press one, to speak with —your current balance is $280.00." Throwing my phone onto the couch, I let out a frustrated grunt. *How the fuck am I going to eat, pay rent, get gas, and everything else for the next fucking week?!*

My body began trembling as I fell to the floor and sobbed. *When did this happen? How did I get to rock bottom?* All I could do was sit on the floor and cry, exhausted from the constant acting and making excuses for everything in life. The thought of *What the hell are you doing with your life?* kept coming up. Over. And over. And over, again.

Ring. Ring. Ring. The sound of my phone ringing snapped me out of my thoughts. The screen read "Ashley R."

"He-l-lo," I blubbered. She asked me how I was doing, and then I lost it even more. She quickly demanded, "What's wrong?!" which only made me cry harder.

Catching my breath, I finally answered her. "What isn't wrong? My life is falling apart, and I don't know what to do about it. I just need something different. I'm tired of this damn town. I'm tired of it all. I need a change of scenery." I heard her exhale, as if she'd been holding her breath the whole time.

"Why don't you move to Texas and live with me?" My heart responded before I could. "Texas? Where? How? When?"

"You can come whenever you want and stay with me. You can stay for free for the first month while you look for work. It's just me and my boyfriend; it won't be a problem. Plus, I miss you and would love to see you every day." She said each word with more excitement than the last.

She was still talking when I drifted away in thought, imagining what it would be like to live in Texas, away from all the bullshit here in Vermont. Suddenly, I was strategizing how I could get there. *What would I bring? Do I drive or fly?*

"Alexis? Are you still there?"

"YES! I'm still here. I was thinking about the logistics of everything. I do want to move to Texas. I'll need to save some money for a few weeks, but then I think I can make it work. Maybe I'll sell my car, work for the next three weeks, and leave at the end of the month." We chatted for another hour, talking about all our plans to have girls' nights, drink wine by the pool, and work together like the old days.

It ended up being six weeks before I left, but I purchased my one-way plane ticket and took the leap of faith to leave and explore the unknown. I worked all my jobs and only went out on occasion to save as much money as I could. Charlene and I traded in bars for parties and cheap fifths of liquor. We spent as much time together as we could throughout that six-week period. I knew I'd miss her more than anyone. She was my first friend when no one else would even look at me; she sat at that cafeteria table despite the social repercussions. Leaving her was bittersweet, but I had to go. I needed something different; I couldn't be there anymore. Life was being sucked away from me with every passing minute. I knew there had to be more, and if there wasn't, at least I could say I tried.

It's crazy thinking about the growth in this season of my life and how I didn't know a thing about personal development, but I was moving through life this way. Taking steps to move from a rut to something better. I wish I could say this is the day everything changed for me and I started on the path I'm on now, but the truth is, I still had no idea what this was. I was finding accidental growth rather than intentional growth. It would be a long time before I'd get to that phase in my life. And as much as I wanted this to work out, it didn't.

On March 9, 2009, I zipped up my last suitcase and headed out the door of Aunt Jen's old house on 2 Colbert Street. The night before, we drank champagne, told stories, laughed, ugly cried, and enjoyed a last moment with my people. They had supported me through it all, and shit was getting real. I was about to leave behind a world I'd only left once before. But this wasn't like when I lived in Massachusetts or Connecticut. No, this was across the country, away from everyone and everything I'd ever known.

My amazing Uncle John called from Afghanistan, where he was stationed, the night before I left to say goodbye. Some of the best advice he'd ever given me was, "Alexis, just know that when you get there, you will get homesick. It might take two weeks, two days, or two months, but don't leave. Call home and talk to the ones you love, and allow yourself to feel that moment, but stay. It will take you at least a year to truly know if you like it, so I challenge you to stay for one year. I know you're going to love it and do extraordinary things."

When something challenges my strength, I don't back down; I stand up. So I told him, "I promise I'll give it at least a year. Thank you, Uncle John, for always seeing more in me than the confinements of Vermont. I love you; talk to you soon!" I hung up that Skype call feeling encouraged and really good about my decision to create a new life.

Aunt Jen drove me to the airport since I had sold my car the day before for extra money. She told me how proud she was of me and to be careful, and then, of course, she told me I didn't have to go. We both laughed and cried, knowing I was getting on that plane and nothing was going to stop me from finding what I was searching for. I couldn't explain it or even describe it, but I felt it deep within my soul. It felt like *hope*.

When we pulled up to the airport drop-off area, I had to get a cart to unpack my four suitcases. And yes, they were over-packed and so dang heavy. My whole life fit into these four red suitcases my mom got me from Avon. I grabbed the last suitcase from the trunk of Aunt Jen's car and hugged her so tightly that neither of us could leave.

"I love you, Aunt Jen. Thank you for everything. I know it's far, but this is going to be so good for me." My voice told a different story than my words, but she knew I had to go. "I'll call you when I get there."

She laughed. "Now I know you're lying because you always forget to call." Through tears and laughter, she said goodbye and gave me one last embrace. From there, I started pushing my cart of suitcases to the desk to check my bags and grab my tickets. With one last look back when I got to the door, I smiled slightly as my heart raced in both excitement and fear. I mouthed "I love you" and crossed the threshold.

You should have seen me strut my way to the counter, partly in a struggle with the heavy-ass cart and partly because I wanted everyone to look at me. I was like, "Hey everyone, I just made a big ole decision to move across the country with a friend I haven't seen in years." This bold move was so courageous for me and something I'd dreamt about my entire life. When I reached the counter, a woman happily greeted me with a warm smile.

"I've got a lot; is that okay?"

"It sure is! Where are you heading, honey?" She listened intently as she checked the bags that I could barely even lift to put on the scale. My last bag was about ninety pounds. *Bloody hell!* And then I choked on air when she said, "That'll be $375, honey. Do you want to pay with cash or card?" This was followed by the most genuinely sweet smile. I handed her four $100 bills and thought to myself, *It's a good thing I sold my car for a couple grand because that would have been my whole budget.*

The plane circled over the San Antonio, Texas, airport upon our descent. I looked eagerly out the window, anticipating the warmth of the sun on my face in my new home. *I'm here, Texas,* I thought to myself as I pulled out my phone. I started writing "I'M HERE!!!!" to text to my girlfriend, Ashley, who I'd be staying with, and hit send the moment we hit the pavement.

She was already at the airport waiting for me, so I went to baggage claim to recover my belongings. The only problem was that the carousel had gone around five and a half times with everything from our plane, and my bags weren't there. Them heffa's decided they were gonna mind my business somewhere else. Rude, if you ask me. So, I found my merry way to customer service and explained my situation.

"I'm so sorry; it looks like your luggage was lost in transit. We'll track them down with your bag tag receipts and bring them to your destination." Her voice sounded like that of a raspy smoker who had just become a bounty hunter, and the grand prize for finding my luggage of life was thousands of dollars.

I was tired from a long layover and flight and didn't see much else I could do, so I headed out to meet Ashley at the car. We headed to the apartment I'd be staying at, for now at least. I had little privacy in the living room, which was uncomfortable since it was Ashley's and her boyfriend's apartment, but I was out of Vermont and ready for change.

About a week in, I really started to miss home, my friends, and familiarity. I didn't have a job yet, so no car and no hope of getting out of this apartment. I loved living with Ashley, but I hated her boyfriend. He was mean to her, and as her best friend, I couldn't sit there and say nothing, even though I probably should have. However, at this point in my life, so much shit had happened that hardened me. I wasn't gentle anymore; I was guarded, angry, and always ready for a fight. I quickly realized, after several arguments and threats, that it was time for me to go. Well, that and he actually told me I had twenty-four hours to leave.

I called my mom since I spent all my money on groceries, money toward bills and clothes, and an entire bed and storage setup. I had to ask her and my stepdad for bus money; I was going to be heading home after a short one-month stay. It was ninety-eight dollars for a ticket from San Antonio, Texas, to Burlington, Vermont. She agreed to Western Union me the money. (If you don't know what this was, think of it like PayPal before PayPal actually existed.)

I decided to call my brother Shawn and tell him I was moving back home. He could hear how disappointed I was since Uncle John said to give it at least a year and I'd failed to make it for more than four damn weeks. His response was to move to Virginia with him, my sister-in-law, and my niece Tristyn.

"I don't know, Shawny; I think I'm just going to go home."

"No, you said you were going to leave and give it at least a year," he said. "If you're already leaving and it hasn't been a year, you might as well come here. It'll be amazing, and I'll set you up with a job at Aaron's since you were supposed to start there in a week." I thought about it and decided, *Why not? I've literally got nothing to lose.*

"Okay, then. Looks like I'm heading to Virginia!" When the call ended, I sent a quick "Thanks, I love you" text and a quick follow-up: "Eeeekkkk. See you in forty-eight hours."

Even though Texas didn't turn out the way I planned, it gave me exactly what I needed: a new direction. When we're paying attention, we can see and follow the doors that open and allow the ones that no longer serve us to close behind us.

Chapter 19

You Were Always My Twin Flame

Do you remember the saying, "If you love something, let it go, and if it returns, it is yours to keep?" That's literally what happened with Dan and me. When I was in Virginia living with my brother, our mutual friend, Lance, kept telling me, "Lex, Danny told me to tell you 'hi' and to write to him." For at least a month, I just rolled my eyes and said, "Probably not." But as it got closer to September 2, 2010, I thought, *Well, I'll write to him for his birthday.* The letter he sent back would change the course of our lives forever.

There's a kind of magic words can't capture—a serendipity too precious to be reduced to letters on a page. But if I had to describe the moment I knew Dan was my twin flame, it would be January 11, 2011, when I came home to Vermont to visit him from Virginia. As luck would have it, it was during one of the most challenging periods (yes, a literal period, actually. Like hey, Aunt Flo, why are you so terrible?) of my life. I'd been bleeding for a year and three months straight (I know, TMI, but I've gotta give you the facts).

Doctors, tests, more doctors—it had been a seemingly endless cycle of bad news and disheartening diagnoses. I tore through a fifty-pack of tampons a week, and my body became a puzzle that even the experts couldn't solve. Doctor after doctor examined me, conducted tests, and shook their heads in confusion.

"You're severely anemic," they concluded, prescribing iron pills that seemed as ineffective as putting water in your gas tank. "It's unlikely you'll ever have kids. If this continues, we'll have to consider a hysterectomy."

Imagine hearing that at twenty-two years young, when your life hasn't even fully started yet. Immediate regret shot through me at the thought of my lost chance at motherhood five years prior. Thinking about the innocent souls I could have embraced tore my heart open at that moment, but this was a well-deserved punishment for the sin I committed.

I was a mess, emotionally, physically, and mentally, but something unexplainable happened—something that only God Himself could have made a reality. I felt a sense of peace as soon as my eyes met Dan's. The world around me melted away. And then, a miracle. When he embraced me, his warmth actually felt as if he healed me, and a little bit later, I went to the bathroom to discover my period had stopped. I thought, *Surely this was not real*, but for the entire eleven days I was with Dan, I had no bleeding. It stopped just like that—no spotting, no cramping, no mood swings. *God, are you messing with me right now?*

You could call it a fluke or divine intervention; I don't have a name for it. But his touch did what modern medicine couldn't. The way his hands warmed my skin felt as though they were repairing a form of inner life—rejuvenation that spread deep into my bones. His embrace was a slice of extraordinary magic in an otherwise harsh time. If there ever was a cure for my sickness, I know it was whatever God put in Dan's touch. My relief was immediate and dramatic. For the first time in over a year, I felt normal. I felt like a woman, not a mystery or a lab rat. I felt... healed.

So here I was, enveloped in the arms of the very first man I ever loved—and, if I'm being honest, never stopped loving. I could feel the hesitance in his touch, questioning if it was real. I looked into his eyes as if to say "Me, too", and we let the gravity of the moment sink in. I felt like I was home. The extraordinary connection between us that had always been there was now intensified by something that defied logic and science. I said a silent prayer, thankful for His kindness and grace toward me when He never had to show me mercy, even when my sins had certainly felt unforgivable.

It was a lot to take in, and the moment I knew this was all a true miracle was when I left Vermont on January 21. After nearly two weeks with Dan, I was left with more questions than answers. Something had happened—something that would require both time and faith to fully understand. It wasn't just a coincidence that my period stopped; it was a spiritual connection so deep that miracles happened. At 2:30 a.m. on January 21, 2011, I went to the bathroom before taking my long twelve-hour journey back to Virginia, and I was met with unbelievable emotions when I realized I started my period... *again*.

I went back home to Virginia, dazed by this experience. I knew I couldn't wait to get back to Vermont and officially start my life with Dan, especially if that meant my cycle might get back on track. It wasn't too long after returning home that I packed up my belongings and headed back to Vermont for good. We moved into our first apartment, where we would come to make tons of memories and experience yet another miracle.

Dan and I continued our relationship. Now that we had found our way back to one another, neither of us was letting go. The day I got to meet Dan's two children officially arrived. The second those little faces appeared in the doorway, my heart was stolen. Jordan and Corine, with their big green and blue eyes and carefree smiles, changed me in a way that I hadn't expected. I didn't know it at the time, but the deep emotional feeling I had that day was unconditional love. One that didn't make sense for a first encounter, but when the plan of God is working out right in front of you, there really is no questioning it.

I mean, I've heard people say there's a difference between loving the children you give birth to and the ones you inherit in a blended family or through adoption. But I had this immediate connection, and I can't relate to that viewpoint. For me, Jordan and Corine broke that theory. These were the beautiful souls who made me a mother for the first time, a role both terrifying and sublime. Given my past experiences and medical challenges, I'd always doubted whether I could be a biological mother, but the moment I met them, I was content knowing that could be a possibility.

The little one-bedroom apartment was always filled with so much love when they were around. It wasn't the perfect setting by any means, but it was ours. Our weekends consisted of living room sleepovers, Saturday morning cartoons, and pancakes drenched in an indecent amount of syrup. Their little laughs became my new favorite melody, and their childlike joy was the most astonishing thing to watch.

One afternoon in our cramped hallway, when Dan, Jordan, and Corine were playing a game of monkey-in-the-middle, their laughter and excitedly loud voices filled the hallway, making it sound as if a hundred people were gathered. I couldn't help but chuckle at them while I made the bed in our room, just to the side of the hallway. Despite the excitement, I started to get a weird instinctive feeling, like a premonition as you'd see on the show *Charmed*.

"Hey, you guys, stop throwing the ball in the hallway, or you'll hit the light," I called from the bedroom.

No sooner had the words escaped my lips when a loud crash echoed through the house. Gasps, then silence. I leaped from the side of the bed as fast as I could. My eyes immediately darted to Corine, who was sitting inches away from the lampshade that fell from the ceiling.

"Corine, don't move, honey, or you'll get cut," Dan and I advised calmly but quickly. He put his sneakers on and grabbed the broom. Corine sat there like a deer in headlights, her eyes widening to their fullest, staring at the shards of our shattered light shade littering the floor. Dan quickly swept up the pieces and picked up Corine to move her away from the glass, while Jordan looked up at me with a "what just happened?" expression.

They all looked at me after the glass was cleaned up, and I just shook my head. A rumble of laughter quickly followed the realization that the warning I'd given and their response, "No, we won't hit it," immediately caused the accident. The irony of the moment was too perfectly timed. They were all okay, and that was what mattered. And I assure you, kickball in the house certainly wasn't played again. That story, on the other hand, is talked about quite often.

Another unforgettable family moment includes Corine's infamous dance recital. Talk about a little girl with sass. To put it bluntly, she hated dance. Not just a little bit; she loathed it.

The curtain lifted, and there she was—our brave, reluctant dancer, standing in the spotlight among her more enthusiastic peers. The music began to play, and the other little girls started their routine. Corine, however, stood there like a statue, defiantly unyielding to the rhythm. Her face? Oh, she wore the meanest mug you could imagine, her tiny features twisted in a blend of rebellion and absolute misery. She refused to move a muscle and refused to smile through what she clearly saw as a torturous ordeal.

When the music finally stopped and the curtain fell, it was abundantly clear to all of us: this was Corine's first and last dance recital. As we left the auditorium, I couldn't help but chuckle at her audacity. What a spirit that sweet girl had. Jordan and I joked with Corine the whole way to their grandparents' house for a BBQ. This was certainly one for the books!

Chapter 20

I Just Peed On That Stick

LIFE as I knew it was about to come to a screeching halt. The doctors kept telling me I would never have children; it just wasn't feasible for me. Well, that didn't stop Dan and I from trying—a lot. It was late March 2011, and I was sitting on my couch doing math homework for my associate degree. In the wee hours of the morning, I decided *that maybe this missed period was more than a weird cycle... Maybe this is it.* I headed into the bathroom, first peeking into our bedroom, where Dan was sleeping like a rock. I tip-toed by.

Sitting on the toilet, I read the instructions one more time. I exhaled deeply and did my best to aim the stick in the line of fire. A bead of sweat trickled down my forehead as if I were in a damn *Mission Impossible* movie, trying not to touch a laser beam. When I was done, I placed the cap back on and set it down. "Don't screw this up," I muttered, almost willing the stick to comply. My phone blinked at 2:02 a.m. Time was up.

I opened my clenched eyes, and there they were: two bright pink lines screaming at me in silence. Suddenly, I found myself on the bathroom floor, struggling to catch my breath. Dramatic? Maybe, but when you're told you can't have children and all of a sudden your prayer is answered, you might be trying to catch your breath, too.

I ran down the hallway, pulled on the lamp's string, and blasted Dan with light. I start jumping up and down directly over him, yelling, "Babe, we're pregnant!" I couldn't contain myself and practically threw the stick at Dan, and it landed directly on his face. He stared at it for a long minute before he said, "Did you just pee on this?" We both immediately burst into laughter. That certainly made it into our Hall of Fame book. We've told our kids that story so many times, and I'm pretty sure it gets funnier each time we tell it.

As my belly and butt expanded, I found myself teetering on the edge like a seesaw. Each morning became a hilarious spectacle of awkward leg swings as I struggled to rise gracefully from bed. It was a nine-month comedy show.

My pregnancy developed with minimal scares and interruptions. We only had one moment of uncertainty that had me in the doctor's office every day for a week. I'm not sure my nervous system had a chance to recalibrate at all that week. As we got closer and closer to the due date, I was so uncomfortable with the biggest belly in the world and nearly tipped over every time I stood up. I started having conversations with the baby inside my belly, Ryan, who was overactive when LMFAO's "Sexy and I Know It" would play. I'm pretty sure he was throwing raves on the daily. I told him he needed to pay rent, and sure enough, he started dropping.

I tried everything that was supposed to make you go into labor, but he was determined to stay. That Christmas, we went to my

Nana's house. After the festivities were over, I had to bring my brother, his wife, and two girls to Shawn's dad's house in St. Alban's for the rest of Christmas. On the way home, it started snowing and, of course, it was dark. My due date was just three days away, and I was nervous I'd be having a baby on the side of the road. Only it wasn't like a Lifetime movie where someone came and rescued me to deliver the baby. I was driving slowly, sliding all over the place, and then I saw them: four deer, crossing the road. I hit my breaks and prayed to God.

"Dear God, don't let me hit this deer and go into labor. Please God, no." On repeat. By the grace of God, I missed all but the tail of the four deer. I bumped his butt, and he was on his merry little way.

I was stopped in the middle of the road when I started hyperventilating, and contractions began. I looked at the clock where I was and realized I still had an hour and fifteen minutes before I'd make it home, and it was turning into a full-blown blizzard. *Why, of all the times I'm driving, does it have to be on Christmas and just three days shy of my due date?* I couldn't get through to Dan's cell, so I called Aunt Jen, who stayed on the phone with me and calmed me while I drove the rest of the way home. I was so stressed out. When I made it safe and sound, I hugged Dan and fell asleep immediately from exhaustion.

The next day, Dan told me about the incoming storm—the worst ice storm we've ever had.

"But I'm due in two days!" I protested. "We need to go into labor and have this baby now." I took him by the hand, went upstairs, and said, "We're not leaving this room until we go into labor." He looked at me really confused, and then I saw it click. With that excitement, we started with the labor-inducing activity that was supposed to be the most fun and effective—making love.

It seemed to work; by 4:30 p.m., my contractions were coming every five minutes. We were watching TV, and as the evening progressed, Dan dozed off, and I thought it was for the best. *Better let him rest*, I thought, breathing through the contractions. *I might need a fully awake chauffeur later.* By midnight, the contractions were getting stronger and closer together. After a quick call to the doctor, I was advised to wait until they were no longer tolerable. Determined not to wake Dan, I powered through three and a half more hours of intensifying pain. Finally, unable to wait any longer, I nudged him awake.

"Babe, we have to go to the hospital. I'm in labor," I announced, my voice as steady as if I were discussing dinner plans.

Disoriented, he jumped up. "Can I make coffee?"

"Sure, but hurry. You have to start the car anyway."

What followed was a blur of motion: Dan darting to the kitchen to brew a pot of coffee, pouring the entire thing into a giant jug, and racing out to start the car. When he came back, I was already downstairs, hospital bag in hand.

That's when he said, "The ice storm started. The snow is falling pretty bad and fast."

He helped me carry the bag to the car and held my arm as we descended the stairs. We got to the car, and when we backed out, the car slid a little, and I immediately had another contraction. "Drive slow," I urged as we cautiously climbed the steep hill leading out of our neighborhood. His hand reached out to touch my shoulder with each bump, as if trying to absorb some of my pain. "Don't touch me," I said as calmly as I could while also trying to focus on my breathing.

In that moment, he switched on the high beams, and rather than illuminate the path, it plunged us into darkness. "What the—?" Dan fumbled with the controls, restoring one dim beam that struggled to cut through the thickening snow. "Our high beams are completely gone! What the fuck?"

By some miracle, we made it to the hospital, where they confirmed my contractions but told me I wasn't dilated enough for admission. Disappointed and in pain, we drove to my mom's house nearby.

Dan headed to work just a couple blocks from Mom's, and I spent hours on all fours, rocking back and forth in an attempt to progress labor. Time was dragging, and the only thing I wanted to do was soak in a bath, so my mom went to run one, only nothing but cold water came out. "Lex, I just called Spates, and they said the city is working on our pipes. We won't have hot water for another couple of hours."

I teared up a little bit but said, "That's okay, I'll be fine." I called the hospital again and told them I couldn't take the contractions anymore. I asked to return to check my progress again. They agreed, so I headed back to the hospital, this time driving myself while in labor. That was interesting.

When we returned to the hospital, this time things were different. As if acknowledging the ordeal we'd gone through just to get there, my body finally started to cooperate. My mom called the worksite to let Dan know we were at the hospital, and that man ran three miles in a blizzard to get to me. Let me tell you, he was a mess when he got there. Luckily, I got a room with a jacuzzi birthing tub and took full advantage. After I weathered twenty-six grueling hours of labor, I opted for an epidural. I just wanted a moment of peace to sleep for just a little bit. But, just my luck, the contractions stopped, and I was only five and a half centimeters dilated.

I was clutching Dan's hand as the doctor said, "The baby's heart rate is dropping. We need to get you into the operating room for a C-section." Dan lost it, completely a mess. My mom consoled him, while I silently made a deal with God that if one of us had to go, it would be me and not this precious baby.

Rushed to the operating room, nurses and doctors moved me around, saying things to me, and before I knew it, I was swallowed by the darkness. When I woke, I found myself in an empty room, aside from a woman at a desk. I looked around frantically, seeing only a light over my bed and the desk that was slightly angled to the side. I tried to sit up, but I was met with extreme pain.

"Am I dead? Where's my baby? Is he okay? Where's my family? Oh, God, what happened?" Loud sobs escaped my mouth, and the nurse rushed to me, telling me everyone was fine. My son was with my husband and family upstairs in the room I'd be taken to shortly. Comforted by these words, I relaxed a bit while she filled me in on the remaining details of what happened. "You and your baby almost didn't make it, but all is well, and everyone is healthy," she said reassuringly.

Motherhood is a jumble of emotions—exhilaration, love, insecurity, and laughable moments. Yet, as I cradled my son in my arms, I realized that being a mother isn't about always knowing the right answers. It's about loving fiercely, nurturing endlessly, and learning alongside this tiny human who has turned my life upside down in the most incredible way.

Just as we were getting the hang of being parents to three beautiful little humans, life decided to throw us another curveball. Aunt Flo, my often-unwelcome monthly visitor, decided to skip her usual appointment. Cue the pregnancy test, the anxious wait, and then—there it was. Those unmistakable two pink lines. We were pregnant *again!*

I mean, Ryan was only nine months old, and the mix of emotions was familiar, but the intensity was on another level. We were just adapting to the chaos and joys of a family of five; how would we manage six? This baby, like each of our children, would bring its own unique joy and challenges into our lives, and I was here for it. And of course, our little big family would rise to the occasion.

Given my previous birthing experience, we decided to opt for a planned C-section this time. I also made the decision to get my tubes tied. It was bittersweet knowing that this would be our last baby, but it was also comforting to have some semblance of control over my own body and future.

The day we welcomed Alexander was filled with emotions, love, and joy. As the surgeon made the incision and lifted him out, his first cry echoed through the room, and it was as if time had stopped. I got to experience childbirth this time. For that single moment, everything was perfect. I looked over at my mom (since Dan and Ryan dipped out to take a nap), her eyes brimming with tears. Dan's face was a blend of joy and relief. I had done it; we were now a family of six.

As they handed Xander to me, after wrapping him in a tiny blanket and placing his small, warm body against my chest, I felt completeness. Dan and I had our ups and downs, navigated through unexpected snowstorms, both literal and metaphorical, and came out stronger on the other side.

Life was good. As I would lie down each night, exhausted but fulfilled, I couldn't help thinking about those pink lines on a test that the doctors said would never show, but by a miracle, it worked out. Life is so beautifully unpredictable, and I was in love with my own perfect slice of heaven.

Chapter 21

Turns Out You're My Romeo

Those storybook fairy tales, where the knight in shining armor would swoop the damsel in distress off her feet, seemed so far away. They existed in movies and books, but never in real life. At least, not in mine.

Until I realized I had the best of them all. My now-husband, a man who saw through my façade of masks and ever-shifting moods, still chose me every single day. When the world saw me strong, he sensed my fragility. And when I insisted I was okay, his embrace reminded me of the safety I had in him. But we were not an immediate fairytale; it took years of work.

Both of us came from troubled pasts. We carried our traumas into the space we occupied together, hoping that love would be the antidote. But it wasn't easy to face the truth: you have to face your demons before you can truly connect with someone. If you think about it, how can you heal someone else when your own wounds are still open?

Our first four years together were intense; our eruptions of past hurts and present insecurities would clash, and we'd end up a little more broken. On the outside, we looked like the epitome of perfection, a couple so in love and so destined because my perfectionism wouldn't allow the outside world to see our weakness. But behind closed doors, we were two broken souls trying desperately to mend one another. However, you can't fix anyone else, only yourself, and that's hard to come to terms with.

Don't get me wrong, our love was intense and powerful, and when he felt the weight of the world pressing down on him, I'd wrap him in an embrace that reminded him we were in it together. And on the days when life threatened to drown me, his touch was my anchor. Yet, our struggles took us to our knees more than once.

One of the darkest chapters in our relationship still stings my heart. There was a time when the walls between us were so thick that I felt his absence even when he was literally inches away from me. We were so disconnected, and I felt like there *had* to be someone else who was driving us apart. These thoughts would create toxic moments and big pockets of distrust. I remember my mom going through my stepdad's things and catching him in lying and cheating. I believed this was the only reason for our disconnect and distance. I accused Dan all the time, invaded his privacy, and tried to puzzle pieces together that simply weren't there. Then he started to do the same to me. We were now each other's worst enemies instead of each other's security.

Every day I woke up next to Dan, I couldn't shake the feeling that I was lying next to a ghost. The man I fell in love with, the man who stood with me on the Grand Union bridge that day, the man I married, seemed to have evaporated, leaving behind a shell burdened with darkness. The depression was like a shroud, concealing the vibrant spirit that had first captivated us. It felt as if we were both sinking in quicksand, pulling each other deeper the more we struggled.

Our house, once filled with laughter and innocent arguments over who cheated in Uno, had turned into an arena, and we were opponents. Our four children were innocent bystanders. Our older two had distanced themselves; maybe they sensed the storm that never seemed to pass, while the younger two still looked at their father as if he hung the moon in the sky. It broke my heart that this was their example of what love was, what marriage looked like, or worse, the example they would think it should be.

We yelled and shouted names that no person should ever call someone they love. Every insult was a lash, and every raised voice was a deepening crack in the foundation of our marriage. I could almost feel the warmth seep out of the scars left behind —emotional wounds that branded us. We had become experts in causing pain; having had so many years of practice, our own childhood traumas were playing out in a cruel cycle we couldn't seem to break.

It was agony to be in a relationship that bore no resemblance to the partnership we thought it would be. It felt like we were playing house, sticking to roles that had long lost their meaning. Roommates in wedding clothes—that was us. Parenting? It was as if we were two actors in separate plays, never sharing the stage but responsible for the same narrative. Our kids deserved better; hell, we both deserved better.

And still, in the silent moments, in the dead of night, when the world paused, my soul cried out for him. I hated the disease that was swallowing him whole, turning him into someone unrecognizable. Every day, I felt like I was losing another piece of myself. I missed my husband, my best friend.

Love was there, buried under years of hurt, misunderstandings, and emotional baggage.

Even in that grim reality, I held on to the glimmers of the man I loved. The way his eyes would momentarily light up watching our youngest take his first steps, the brief smile that crossed his lips when I made his favorite meal. Those fragments reminded me that somewhere inside that troubled man was my Dan, fighting to come back, just as I was fighting to find a way to reach him.

I couldn't help but hope for the bridge to reappear between us—a connection to reverse the widening gap between us. Our love story wasn't over; it was just stuck, in need of a new chapter, one that I prayed every night would somehow write itself. And though that chapter seemed elusive—an unwritten page in a story that had veered off course—I held onto the belief that love, in its most authentic, messy, complicated form, was strong enough to rewrite even the most painful narratives. It had to be; it was what kept me going.

As I lay in our bed contemplating how we got here, I recalled the day in 2014 when Dan was diagnosed with ulcerative colitis. It felt like the day we both received a life sentence. We had already been grappling with his deepening depression, and unbeknownst to me and the rest of the world, mine was brewing too. This was a physical manifestation, an undeniable reality we couldn't argue away or wish into nonexistence. The once vibrant, charismatic Dan, the boxer and MMA fighter—the man everyone in town saw as a hero—was now reduced to a bedridden shell of himself, plagued by constant pain.

I tried to lift his spirits the only way I knew how: by planning trips, family outings, or anything else to awaken the man who used to relish life's adventures. But each time, he'd look at me with sad eyes and decline, and my heart would break a tiny bit more. He'd say, "I don't want to be a burden." His disease made him feel like less than the man he was, and it shattered my heart to see him so diminished.

Life just went on around us in a twisted parody of normalcy. I was juggling a full-time job, school, and carting the kids to daycare, becoming the sun around which our small universe revolved. It felt like I was forced to fill the roles of both parents, both partners, and both confidants. I became the rock, the organizer, and the perpetual motion machine that kept our lives on track, but at an immense emotional cost.

Eventually, the weight of being everything to everyone became too much to bear. I could no longer be the punching bag, the fixer, or the eternal optimist who plastered a smile on her face while her insides crumbled. One evening, I finally broke. I moved my belongings into the spare bedroom, shutting the door not just on a room but on a chapter of our lives that had caused us both so much pain.

Sleeping alone, I found myself crying into the silence, missing the man who lay just a hallway away, yet miles apart in spirit. I watched him go out a couple of nights, not knowing where he went or if he'd come back, each absence a silent confirmation of my deepest fears—I was no longer enough for him. Or worse, maybe I never had.

But then, something happened. Pulling myself out of his orbit seemed to jar something loose in him and me. It's as if my withdrawal made him finally see the void we created. The man who had given up on living suddenly found a reason to come back to life. Yet the irony was crushing. My soul, anchored to his for so long, felt like it had floated away, leaving behind an emptiness so profound that no one even noticed its absence.

I'd reached a crossroads. I still wanted to be a wife, a lover, and a companion, but not at the expense of losing myself. I wanted to earn my degree, build a career, and be more than just the glue holding everyone else together. And more than anything, I wanted to love Dan, to stand by him through his battle, as he had once stood by me on that bridge all those years ago when no one else saw me. But this time, it had to be different. This time, we both had to want to cross that bridge together, taking steps toward a middle ground where love, in all its complicated, painful, but ultimately redeeming glory, could flourish again.

As I stood at the kitchen sink, washing dishes on autopilot, my thoughts spiraled into a void. I thought about the verbal volleys Dan and I had exchanged over the years: the harsh words, the accusations, and the daggers we'd thrown that could never be taken back. In that moment, I felt an emptiness so deep that even the air around me seemed empty of life.

A single tear escaped and traced a path down my cheek, as if it had been waiting for permission to release the flood behind it. I barely noticed Dan walking into the kitchen, and his words were just sounds that didn't form meaning in my ears. Until he said something that penetrated through my armor and settled around my spirit.

"I'm so sorry. I didn't realize just how much I'd hurt you until right now," he said through a tight throat and tears. "You look so empty, and I'm so sorry. I'll do better; I want us to do better."

His words were like a lifeline thrown into the murky waters where I'd been drowning. For the first time in a long while, I felt seen, truly seen, in all my pain and imperfection. I cried. I cried hard, the tears coming as if a dam had burst within me. I felt like a desert suddenly nourished by a long-awaited rain. But what surprised me the most in that moment was not the relief of my tears but the sudden rekindling of something I'd almost forgotten—*hope*.

I couldn't muster the strength to say anything, so I just stood there, letting my tears speak the volumes that words had failed to convey. And for the first time in a long time, I felt like maybe, just maybe, the life we had torn down had a chance to be rebuilt, piece by fragile piece.

Those tears, mingling with the dishwater, felt like a cleansing of more than just ceramic and glass. They felt like the first drops in a season of renewal that both Dan and I so desperately needed. It was as if we were washing away the years of grime and resentment that had built up between us, making way for something new and yet hauntingly familiar—the raw, unfiltered love that had first drawn us to each other.

It wasn't a magical cure-all. There were still miles to go, mountains of past hurts to climb, and rivers of forgiveness to wade through. But at that moment, the journey seemed possible, even if the path would be laden with thorns and obstacles. Because now, at least, we could see that the only way out of the maze we'd trapped ourselves in was to walk through it together.

I wish I could say I was the innocent victim in all this, a martyr caught in the vortex of her struggles. But that would be a lie. I'd lashed out in my own ways many times, letting my anger and resentment boil over into words that I could never unsay. We were two people caught in a vicious cycle, both inflicting wounds while nursing our own. It was a dynamic that left us both broken but still inexplicably tethered to each other.

I had expected him to "snap out of it" and to just love me the way I thought love should look, not realizing that he was mourning an entire identity that was stolen from him. He'd lost so much more than physical strength; he'd lost a lifetime of dreams and self-worth that he'd built around his physical abilities. And there I was, ignorant of his silent existential crisis, angrily wondering why he couldn't just be happy and why he couldn't just be there for *me*.

The truth is, we were both wrong, and we were both right. We were two flawed people trying to find our way through a thicket of past hurts, misunderstandings, and an insidious illness that seemed to rob us of everything we'd known to be true about ourselves. But here's the thing I hold onto the most: we never gave up on each other. And that's the only reason we're still here—still us.

Within a month of that tearful night at the kitchen sink, I started therapy. My therapist became the guiding force I didn't realize I needed. She helped me understand that it wasn't just about what I was going through but also about understanding what Dan was experiencing. She gave me the tools to foster genuine communication between us, to facilitate healing not just within me but in our relationship. This work was done over a period of seven years, but I started seeing results from my willingness to be open and do the work in the first year.

Today, some of my favorite memories are the ones we've created since that turning point. They're not grand or spectacular in the way that movies often portray love; they're quiet moments filled with shared laughter, small victories in our struggle to be better people, partners, and parents, and, yes, sometimes they're about navigating the uncomfortable discussions most would shy away from. You have to be willing to deal with shit to get back on track.

He's my person, and I'm his. And in a world that often feels heavy, that's a bit of everyday magic I won't ever take for granted. We found our way back to each other through the chaos, like two stars lost in the vast universe that found their way home. And so we continue, hand in hand, in the journey through both the storms and clear skies that life has in store for us. And more importantly, we remember where we've been and speak up when we're off. And best of all, we are willing to try to shift behaviors when one of us is vulnerable enough to say, "That hurts."

In that bleak period, life seemed like a surreal, slow-moving dream. Every step felt heavy, and every smile was forced. But a tiny ember of hope flickered until we put our focus into making it a flame again. Dan's determination, the rawness of his love, refused to let go. And I, realizing the depths of my feelings, started to fight, too. We realized together that our fight is unstoppable, gritty, and filled with passion. We were certainly stronger together.

Our love story isn't one of endless romance; it's about resilience. It's about finding strength in vulnerability and understanding that true love isn't the absence of pain but the commitment to push through it together.

Today, after countless battles, we stand tall. We're still learning, evolving, and healing. And yes, love is fragile. But in its fragility lies its strength. Because while love can be hurt, broken, and tested, it also has the power to heal, mend, and win.

Chapter 22

What Will It Take

For as long as I can remember, my life has been a nonstop treadmill of high expectations, to-do lists, and constant motion. People often called me an overachiever, but that was an understatement. I was more than just diligent; I was obsessive, possessed by the notion that I needed to do more, achieve more, and be more. Perhaps it was my high-functioning anxiety, or maybe it was the ADHD that always kept my thoughts racing at a million miles a minute. It was impossible for me to focus if I wasn't juggling a dozen tasks at once. But above all, it was a deep-seated belief that my worth, my lovability, and my place in the world were directly tied to my achievements.

For years, I took pride in being a workaholic. I wore my perpetual exhaustion like a badge of honor. My job in a toxic work environment didn't help. The air was thick with tension, but instead of looking for a way out, I leaned in. I poured every ounce of myself into my work, sacrificing weekends, family time, and even my health, believing that my relentless effort would validate me. It was a desperate, endless cycle, and I kept spiraling, refusing to listen to the alarm bells ringing in the form of both mental and physical distress.

The first wake-up call was Bell's palsy. One day in February 2020, I looked in the mirror, and half of my face was frozen—a numb mask. The sight was terrifying, and it was a physical manifestation of all the emotional and mental paralysis I'd been feeling. But that wasn't enough to stop me.

The hits kept coming. Next was the thyroidectomy the following month, a grueling surgical procedure that left me bedridden and faced with a lifetime of medication. It seemed that my body was shouting at me now, urging me to stop and evaluate my life and choices. Did I listen? I tried, but the noise of my demanding job and my own fears drowned out those desperate cries from within.

Then came the second part of the hysterectomy in July 2021. At this point, the message was loud and clear: my body couldn't take this lifestyle anymore. Each surgical scar became a physical marker of my negligence towards myself, and I couldn't ignore it any longer. But it wasn't just about me; I had to consider the toll my workaholism and health issues were taking on my family. *How could I be present as a mother or wife when I was barely present for myself?*

That's when it dawned on me. My desperate race to validate my worth had only devalued me. I had traded my well-being for a toxic illusion of success and recognition. The cost was devastating, and no job or achievement was worth the price I had paid.

So, I began the journey of unlearning. I took a step back to reassess what really mattered in my life. Slowly, I set boundaries, limited my work hours, and, most importantly, tuned into what I needed internally. I discovered modes of healing that included embracing therapy and practices for my ADHD and anxiety, no longer seeing them as signs of weakness but as tools for betterment.

It has been a hard road, full of challenges and pitfalls, but I've come to realize that the first step towards healing is admitting that you're hurt. And the first step toward success is defining what it truly means for you, away from the noise of the world and the chaos of a restless mind.

As I write this chapter of my life, I can't undo the choices I've made or the medical obstacles I've faced. What I can do is write a new narrative—one where my value isn't measured by my productivity or societal validation but by the love and peace I find within myself. And that, for the first time, feels like a true achievement.

As I settled into a routine of self-care and reevaluation, it was impossible not to think about the collateral damage my workaholic tendencies had caused. The first casualties, of course, were those closest to me: my family. My spouse, the rock of our family, often looked drained, as if he were carrying the weight of the world alone. And in a sense, he was. I was physically there but emotionally distant, always on my phone or laptop, never really present.

And then there were my kids. Oh, the countless bedtime stories I missed, the recitals, the simple, beautiful act of tucking them into bed—all sacrificed at the altar of my career. The worst part was that they were getting used to it and were no longer surprised when Mommy couldn't make it. They were resilient, yes, but at what cost? My guilt was unbearable.

Missing those key moments was like missing pieces of my own soul—pieces I could never get back. The irony wasn't lost on me; I was working and studying to provide a better life "for them," and yet, they were growing up without fully having me in their lives. How could I claim to be doing it all for my family if I was absent from the very moments that made a family whole?

The memory of the birthday I missed haunts me to this day. I remember receiving pictures on my phone—photos that I took a quick glance at before going back to work. My child's face lit up in joy, a joy I didn't witness firsthand. And the first steps—those *irreplaceable* first steps? I saw them in a video, not in person. They happened without me, and they'd keep happening without me unless I made a change.

I was going to school at the same time, always rationalizing the chaos as a necessary evil. But what was the endgame? To graduate, to get a higher-paying job, to keep climbing that ladder? What would be enough if the people I was doing this for were falling by the wayside? It was a bitter pill to swallow. My family was getting an empty vessel of a mother and wife, an automated version of me that functioned but didn't truly live.

Autopilot had become my default setting. I was navigating through life, but not really experiencing it. My body was there, but my mind and soul were miles away, locked up in to-do lists, deadlines, and never-ending responsibilities. Meanwhile, my children were missing their mom, the woman who was supposed to be their rock, their nurturer, and their biggest fan. My spouse was missing his partner in life—the woman he decided to share his dreams, joys, and even mundane moments with.

The ripple effects of my high-strung, frenetic lifestyle didn't stop at home; they spread like wildfire through my professional life, too. As the team leader, I had set the tone for our work culture, and it was far from healthy. Sure, we were productive, hitting our targets and even exceeding them, but I could see the strain in my team's faces during meetings. They were emulating me, thinking this is what leadership looks like and this is how you succeed. In reality, I was teaching them the best way to burn out, to alienate their loved ones, and to ignore their needs —lessons I wouldn't pass on to my worst enemy.

If your team reflects your leadership, then mine was a mirror I had avoided looking into for far too long. The stress, the endless hours, and the unmanageable expectations—they were all manifesting in the way my team interacted with each other and how they managed their own workloads. I had to face the harsh reality: my skewed version of "success" had not only impacted my well-being but had created a toxic environment for the people I was responsible for.

When I finally looked in the mirror, I didn't recognize the woman staring back at me. It was a moment of reckoning. I had become so disconnected from my own life that the people I loved the most were getting used to my absence, both physically and emotionally. That's when I knew I had to reevaluate what mattered. It wasn't an overnight transformation; those never last. It was a daily choice to be present, to slow down, and to prioritize.

I started by being honest, first with myself and then with my team. I began to open up about my struggles and my realization that we were headed down a dangerous path. I encouraged them to rethink our priorities, to focus on quality over quantity, and to remember that our jobs are just one part of our lives, not the sum total of our identity.

And as for me, I went back to the drawing board. My definition of success now involves a balanced life where my family comes first, where my health isn't compromised, and where my team feels supported, not burdened, by my leadership. It's a work in progress, but aren't we all?

I now find joy in the small moments—reading a bedtime story to my kids, enjoying a quiet dinner with my spouse, even laughing genuinely during a team meeting. I'm learning to appreciate these snippets of time as the true milestones of a life well lived. And for the first time in a long time, that feels like enough.

Now, I'm learning to shake off that auto-pilot mode and to engage with the world around me, starting with my own family. I'm learning to listen, not just hear; to look, not just see; and to feel, not just touch. Every day, I'm choosing to be present, and while I'll never get back the moments I missed, I can make sure I'm there for the ones that are still to come. One day at a time.

Chapter 23

You Have What It Takes

It's funny how life works. For the longest time, I was stuck in a loop of self-destruction, and then a job at Cumbie's—the kind of job people don't think twice about—became my unlikely salvation. It was there that I learned the first lessons in self-respect and resilience. It also taught me another invaluable lesson: life isn't about getting what you want; it's about becoming someone who will go after what you want.

Fast forward to 2020, a year of unprecedented challenges but also new beginnings for me. This time, I aimed higher, much higher. I applied to join our local state police department. Talk about a total one-eighty, right? To even think of entering law enforcement was way out of my comfort zone, but I needed to prove to myself that I could do it.

Receiving the acceptance letter for the initial testing was a burst of triumph I'll never forget. It validated that I was more than my past, more than my mistakes. The requirements scared me, touching on every area where I lacked confidence—educational ability, physical strength, and truthfulness. But I wanted this, and that desire was a seed of change.

I drove three and a half hours to get to the academy site, where the energy of thousands of trained and graduated state troopers lingered in the air. I could almost picture myself among them—uniform crisp, face determined, shoulders back. That vision intensified as I parked my car. Hell, I was the first one there. I couldn't afford to mess this up. Whether it was a flat tire or a fuel issue, I had to prepare for every obstacle.

Before I went inside, I prayed in my car for the strength to get through all the phases of the testing, especially the written exam. My Achilles' heel has always been performance anxiety. It doesn't matter how much I prepare; the moment I'm faced with that booklet and answer sheet, my mind turns into an echoing void. But I had my study cards, my prep tests, and my books flagged with colorful sticky notes—more preparation than I had ever put into my entire time at Southern New Hampshire University for my bachelor's degree. This time, I wanted not just to pass but to crush it, to show the world and myself that I could do it.

Whether or not I achieved that goal wasn't the point. What mattered was that I was stretching myself, challenging years of self-doubt, trauma, and fear. The journey itself became a lesson, a chapter in a story that I am still writing. And in that chapter, I found something invaluable—a little more strength, a little more confidence, and a whole lot of determination to keep going, no matter what.

I walked into that gym, and I could feel every thump of my heartbeat echoing in my ears. Each beat seemed to ask, "Are you ready? Can you do this?" Without hesitating, my soul whispered back, *Yes*. The room was filled with rows of tables and chairs—all aligned in the rigor of uniformity. At that moment, I felt aligned too, determined, ready, and prepared.

My hand moved across the answer sheet, filling in the bubbles as quickly and accurately as I could. Every tick of the clock was a reminder, both of how far I had come and how much further I still had to go. When the time was up, I had five minutes to spare—a lifetime in a setting like this.

We all filed outside, sitting on the grass, lost in the world of our thoughts, pondering what the immediate future held. They called seven of us back inside to receive our results. *Seven out of a hundred,* I thought. *Not great odds.* Yet I still walked back in, head held high.

Aaron, the recruiter, gave me a sort of smile. "You did really well, but you just missed the minimum score by one point," he said, almost apologetically. He suggested I come back to retest in two weeks. That sucked, but there was no way I was going to let that setback define me.

Two weeks later, I was back—hungrier and more prepared than ever. I scored eighty-two percent, twelve points above the requirement and the highest in the room! Next came the physical tests, where I ranked second. Then the email for the interview process came within forty-eight hours. The polygraph followed, which felt like an interrogation of not just my honesty but my entire life. I passed, receiving a contingent offer letter.

Another two weeks passed, and it was time for the results. I tore open the letter, my heart pounding. "It was a tough decision," it read. "With limited space for only twenty-two, you fell just outside of our cut-off. Thank you for your interest, time, and effort. We wish you the best."

I was crushed. At that moment, the letter felt like one more piece of evidence for my inadequacy. But then, after some time to grieve, I realized something: I had stretched beyond limits I never knew I could reach. I had walked through a gauntlet of challenges I'd never dared face before, and I'd come out the other side, not beaten but better.

So yeah, I allowed myself to sit in the hurt for a bit. I mourned that missed opportunity, the could-have-beens, the work, the sweat, and the hours of study. But then I moved past the disappointment and embraced the lessons, the growth, and the journey that led me there. I didn't get what I wanted, but I got something potentially more valuable—a deeper understanding of my resilience and of my ability to bounce back from defeat. I didn't become a state trooper, but I became a stronger, more focused, and more determined version of myself.

And that, *that* is the victory.

For weeks, the atmosphere at home, among friends, and even at family gatherings was thick with pity, sympathy, and, at times, indignation. Everyone seemed to feel my failure as keenly as if it had been their own, but in a very different way. "How could they do this to you?" "You were so close!" "They don't deserve you."

But, you see, the most impactful part of my journey wasn't the moment I opened that disappointing letter. No, it was the time after that when I rose from that stumble with more grace and resolve than I had ever known I possessed.

So, one evening, I sat my kids down. They had sensed something was off and, in the way children do, absorbed the emotional shifts around them. Their eyes met mine, wide and questioning.

"Kids," I began, "Mommy worked really hard for something, something she really wanted. But she didn't get it."

"Why not?" my youngest asked, his voice tinged with confusion.

"That's just how life is sometimes," I said. "But you know what? Even though Mommy didn't get what she wanted, she got something better."

Their eyes widened. "What's better than getting what you want?"

I smiled, taking a moment to let the weight of the conversation settle in. "Learning that it's okay to fail. Learning that sometimes the journey—the hard work, the discipline, the late nights, and the effort—is more important than the destination. And I experience so much growth in my belief in my ability to do things I really want to do. And so can you!"

The beauty of this teaching moment went beyond my family; it rippled through my circle of friends and extended family. I made sure to openly share my new perspective. I began to notice a shift in conversations, away from pity and resentment and steering towards admiration for the courage it took to even attempt such a feat.

"You went for it, and that's more than most of us can say," a friend told me one day.

And it was true. I had leaped far out of my comfort zone. For the first time, I'd aimed for something big, something risky, something that demanded every ounce of courage and resilience I had. And though I had aimed for the moon and landing among the stars, it was the journey through the night sky that mattered most.

I used this experience as a platform to dispel the myth of perfection, normalize failure, and celebrate the brave endeavor of aiming high, even when the target seems impossibly out of reach.

When all was said and done, I had not only learned one of life's most valuable lessons but had also found a way to pass it on to the people who mattered most to me. I taught them that life's true victories sometimes look a lot like defeat and that the taste of failure can be the first step towards a life more enriching and enlightening than we ever thought possible.

And that, in the end, was my true success.

Chapter 24

My Heart Is My Superpower

I WENT from being masked and like a caged animal to being set free. It's funny how when you listen to God and allow Him to guide you, your perspective shifts. Life is no longer a race to become something specific or shapeshifting for someone, but rather, to become the woman God intended me to be.

I've shouldered a lot of burdens over the years, but this is truly where it all begins. The day that you decide enough is enough and change is around the corner. To *become* is the phase in which you dare greatly, take chances, and allow yourself to be lost in the world of indifference. That's my power; that's what God gave me.

So on this journey of becoming this powerful version of me, I've challenged myself to look back at all the things I've endured—the pain, the loss, the excitement, the joy—and blend them all together into life lessons, guidance, and wisdom. My heart is my superpower; the love that I give and share is the light that people talk about that radiates for me when I walk into a room. That's difficult to articulate without feeling as if I'm being conceited, but truly, this is what I've realized over the years. When people talk about my presence and the light that glows within me when I walk into a room, my heart is what that light makes them feel. It's amazing when you begin to love yourself and suddenly feel your own radiation, too.

I am standing in my power, firmly grounded in the essence of who I am and what I stand for. It's a conviction that has come to me not easily, but through a painstaking journey of self-discovery, a journey fought with detours and obstacles that, more often than not, were of my own making. Now, I am the girl whose voice doesn't quiver in the face of adversity or surrender to the looming shadows of her past. Instead, I've learned to harness those shadows and transmute their once crippling darkness into a force that propels me forward. Each shadow is but a fragment of the light I hold within, a light that I am destined to shine upon the world. I am no longer bound by the spells of my past but freed by the power of my present and the promise of my future.

I am becoming the person God envisioned when He sculpted me from mere stardust and breathed the essence of life and a beam of hope into me, a living testimony to the power of the human spirit. As I embrace this transformation, I understand that "becoming" is not a destination but an eternal journey, one that I will navigate with the courage birthed from the mountains I've climbed and the battles I've endured throughout my life.

I am becoming love, for it's in love that I find my truest expression and my deepest resonance. I am becoming change, a living embodiment of the transformation that's possible when one dares to take that first courageous step toward authenticity and vulnerability. I am becoming stronger, fueled by the wisdom of my experiences and fortified by the grace of my revelations.

I am becoming me.

In May 2022, I took a leap of faith. A contest application for a trip to the Know Women Summit blinked at me from my screen. It was a Hail Mary, to be honest, but I filled it out with a sort of nonchalant courage. *If I win, amazing! If not, that's cool, too!* I thought. Imagine my disbelief when, just twenty-four hours later, an email arrived proclaiming I'd won! The rush of excitement was immediate, only to be overshadowed by a creeping sense of terror. *Arizona? An empowerment conference? What had I gotten myself into?*

But when God commands the universe to nudge you, you listen. Right?

I reached out to Darcey, the person who had shared the post about the contest. We'd only met a couple of times via Zoom calls a few years before. Yet, I felt pulled to ask her, so I sent her a voice memo.

"Do you want to come with me to the Know Women's Summit? We can share a room."

Less than a minute passed before I received her reply, "YES!!"

Later that day, we discovered that Jamie Kern Lima would be one of the speakers. I couldn't believe it! The founder of IT Cosmetics, the author of "Believe It," a book I'd just recently devoured that had changed everything about how I viewed my obstacles. The universe wasn't just nudging me; it was shoving me toward a destiny I'd not yet fully comprehended.

Attending that summit was like stepping into a dream, or maybe, more precisely, stepping out of a cocoon. With every speaker I heard, every woman I met, and every potent conversation I had, I felt layers of self-doubt and inhibition falling away. I became someone I had never met before—a woman filled with confidence, buzzing with excitement, and absolutely ready to take on the world.

I remember standing there, filled with anticipation, with my heart pounding in my chest as Jamie Kern Lima concluded her riveting talk. The applause around me was deafening, but all I could think of was the chance to meet her, to look her in the eyes, and simply say, "Thank you."

I moved towards the stage, navigating through the crowd, and for a split second, our eyes met. Just as I was about to extend my hand, the host took her arm and whisked her away for some immediate obligation. The proximity to my role model, just inches away, made the missed connection even more agonizing. I felt as if the universe had dangled a life-changing moment in front of me, only to yank it away.

I was crushed. Retreating to a corner, I let the tears flow. This was more than just a missed opportunity; it was a missed connection to thank someone who had ignited a fire in me when I was drowning in darkness. Her book had been a divine intervention, appearing in my life precisely when I'd prayed for guidance.

But every end is a new beginning, so I decided to pray about reaching out to Jamie on Instagram. I sought the kind of celestial counsel that had never led me astray. Then, after weeks of contemplation, I decided to take another leap. I composed a message for her. It was a message from the heart, filled with vulnerability and the kind of raw honesty that you can't just make up. I told her everything I had wanted to say that day and hit send, leaving it to the cosmos.

And then magic happened.

Less than forty-eight hours later, my phone buzzed with a notification. A voice memo from Jamie herself. My hands trembled as I pressed play. Her voice filled the room, thanking me for my message and sharing her own words of encouragement. It was an act of kindness so selfless and so utterly generous that it left me speechless.

She didn't have to respond. She could have easily ignored the message, buried under the weight of her many responsibilities. But she didn't. And now, whenever I find myself doubting or questioning my path, I listen to her message again. It's as if God has chosen to speak through her words, to remind me of the larger picture being created, stitch by stitch, experience by experience.

And so, whenever I think back to that day at the summit, to the moment I stood inches away from Jamie yet worlds apart, I smile. I now realize that the universe was never playing a cruel joke; it was setting the stage for a more profound connection, a lesson in patience, perseverance, and the incredible power of gratitude. It's a reminder that even when you think you've missed your moment, sometimes the universe has an even better one waiting just around the corner.

On top of that, Darcey and I became more than just summit buddies. Our conversations were transformative, packed with the kind of vulnerability that makes your voice tremble and your heart race. We talked about our fears, our goals, and our wildest, most unreachable dreams, which suddenly began to feel not so unreachable after all. We found a cadence of communication that turned into daily check-ins, business brainstorming sessions, and moments of raw emotional honesty both of us had been craving. Our friendship blossomed into a beautiful relationship, nurtured by authentic connection and mutual growth.

And here's the thing: this was just the beginning. This was the opening act of a journey of becoming. Becoming undeniable, becoming unstoppable, and becoming the light that casts out shadows not just in my world but in the worlds of those around me.

This is not just my story; it's our story. It's a story of what happens when you leap when you listen to that still, small voice telling you to take the risk. It's a story of transformation, not just in who you are but in what you believe is possible.

So if you're standing on the edge of a decision, an opportunity, or even just a simple contest application, take the leap. You never know where you'll land, but I promise you this: the journey will be nothing short of extraordinary.

Chapter 25

Shattered Reality

I'VE BEEN HIDING my identity and trying to become somebody that everybody wanted to be around—somebody that was appealing to the wrong audience. Somebody that was the yes girl, somebody that was perfect, somebody that immersed herself in work. I became an achiever and a winner, and I lost myself.

The day was October 3, 2022, when my family got the call.

"Your son was in an accident on his motorcycle."

The panicked look on my husband's face when he scrambled to get his shoes on because only one of us could go running out the door. My vision was distorted. I paced the living room back and forth, trying to figure out what was happening. My stomach turned, so I went upstairs to the bathroom because I was freaking out. I had no idea what to do, what to say, or what to think—crippled by fear, not for myself but for somebody that I love so deeply.

I got another call twenty-five minutes later. I heard his screams on the other end. *What are you saying?* I couldn't comprehend it; all I heard was, "They took our boy; they took our boy."

That broke me for the rest of my life.

That was the moment I had to sit with. We will never get another hug, another "I love you," another "goodbye, see you later," or a movie night with the Sour Patch watermelon candies we all loved so much. Too much. I can't do this life anymore. I can't do the hustle. I can't prioritize everything that I love. Some might even argue that I didn't prioritize my family at all. I realized in that moment that *this very second* is all I have. All I will ever have. Five minutes from now, I could collapse from a heart attack.

I could have a stroke. I could be hit by a car. Whatever the scenario is, I don't know what happens five minutes from now, but the thing that I do know is what happens right now, in this very moment; this second of my life is what I know to be true.

Fear will cripple us until the day we die, if we let it. I realized at that time that I'd been holding onto my story for so long, and the crazy thing is that when you hold onto your story, it holds power over you. And so I started writing.

I'd actually begun writing my story a year prior to that. I had reached out to one of my mentors, Lindsey, and asked her if she had any recommendations for writers. She introduced me to one of the most impactful people who would change my life. This woman rooted for *me* to believe in *me* so deeply; to not allow *me* to give up on myself. Her name is Lauren Eckhardt.

Lauren is my book coach and the publisher of my story.

I wrote my story to be dedicated to my son, Jordan.

I wrote my story to be dedicated to the family that I will no longer choose to leave behind.

I wrote my story for a little seven-year-old Alexis, for that scared little girl who didn't know who to be. I gave her a life, I gave her a voice, and I gave her a transition into who we are today because of the sacrifices and choices that we made during a time of survival. Now, we can use our story to inspire others to do the same; we don't need to choose fear.

Today I am the published author of a book called *Changing the Reflection: The Faces We Wear and the Truths They Hide*. I chose that title because I knew I could never change my past.

I could never, ever choose to be anybody other than who I am today. We can change the reflection we see at any time. We can surround ourselves in healthy environments and with people who understand our future vision. We can be loved by people who will hold space for our story, and if they don't, we're in the wrong circle.

On July 26, 2023, I got a call at 11:30 p.m. The now familiar fear and anxiety of an unexpected phone call sank in again because my Nana never calls me that late at night. The first person to go through my mind was my mother. The second person to go through my mind was my brother. Then the list went on and on. Who could they be calling about? Is somebody hurt? Is everybody okay? Then, I noticed the missed notifications: ten missed calls from my mom, eight voicemails, and text messages from every family member.

Another call came through, which I picked up. It was Uncle Jr. calling to let me know that he was so sorry my brother was gone. It took me a minute to comprehend what he was saying to me. His words didn't quite make sense. *Gone? Gone where?*

Shawny had gone to prison again a couple of days before—forty-eight hours, to be exact. He was found in the bathroom, on the ground, when the guards found him, where the paramedics tried to revive him.

Were they a minute too late? Ten minutes too late? Two seconds too late? I don't know what his last moments looked like. What I do know is that my brother lied there on the ground, scared, alone, and by himself, because he was so deeply ashamed. He carried guilt and sorrow nobody saw; they just saw somebody they would call a drug addict, a criminal. Somebody who wasn't worthy of their time to care about.

He was my hero. For as long as I can remember, he protected me from everything—*always*. When we were kids in an abusive foster home, he would protect me. When our mom was less than loving to me, he would love me harder. When the police and social services came to take us because our mom was still in rehab, I only had my brother. Instead of being a little kid, he was my guardian, my adult at five years old, trying to help me survive. Shawny stepped up to take on responsibilities no five-year-old child should ever carry. But he did it because he loved me.

My only regret is that I had been a better little sister on that holiday when the roads seemed like they were too bad to travel. They probably weren't, and we missed Christmas at his house, which would've been my last Christmas with him. The year after that, we skipped Christmas; we traveled, but with just our children, mourning our son that we had just lost.

I look back at the calls and text messages from my brother. "I would love to start doing family dinners." "Can we plan a time, maybe a day, even once a month, to sit down and just love each other?" "I miss you, sis." We talked for hours that day. I told him how much I missed him, too, and I loved the idea of getting together. We could just enjoy each other's company and laugh, joke, and play. The kids would get together and love each other and build that cousin bond like what we had with our family.

Life got really dark for him, and he thought that he had to do it alone. He turned to his vessel to numb the pain, which was drugs for him (alcohol for me). But then it consumed him, enveloped him in the darkness, and then he was no longer here. All of these things flashed through my head again.

How? Why? I thought I was doing better. I thought I was being more intentional with my time. *We just lost Jordan; this can't be real.* My heart crumbled into dust.

I dragged my feet with my book. I had the outline done; I just needed to do a few touch-ups and some edits and get it to Lauren. We were going to discuss the publishing phase soon, and the message that I got *again was*: stop hiding yourself, be present, and take the time. I realized I was hiding again; even though I was so deeply wounded and felt closer to my family and more intentional, I still wasn't. I was wasting time. I was scared, allowing fear and anxiety to take over, and that day I refused to take more time.

I believed the universe nudged me again, saying, "I tried to warn you in other ways, but you just wouldn't listen. I need you to stop hiding. There are people you need to help. Time is precious. Learn the lesson this time."

FUCK! I don't want to lose another person over this. I can't take any more losses in my life. I prayed to God like I've never prayed before. Three days later, I got the phone call that Aunt Maggie passed away, and I got the message again.

"You're not listening. I need you to be present. I need you to stop hiding and unmask yourself. I need you to remember that *now* is the only time you have. I had to teach you because you won't listen."

I prayed to God, and I said, "Lord, I cannot lose any more people. What do you need me to do? Tell me what you need me to do, and I will do it because I cannot handle another loss in my life. I get the message."

Again, He said, "Stop hiding; unmask yourself; be present."

"Lord, that's what I'm trying to do. Tell me how to do it." And I was forced to plan my brother's funeral and take on financial expenses. He deserved it, and he would've done it for me. I asked my kids what they wanted to do and what they needed from me. They only asked for hugs.

They showed me love and affection. They asked me to watch a movie, and I felt a little piece of hope in my heart. After so much tragedy, it's hard to see through the fog, but if you become still and allow yourself to pause, things can turn around.

I had people who had known me for a very short amount of time, Jen Gottlieb and Chris Winfield in particular, check on me during this time. I still don't even think they fully understand the capacity with which I hold them in my heart. For them to love me and to support me through the loss of somebody they didn't know was nothing short of incredible. They reminded me that I was important and that the world needed to see me. They were there for me, and they wanted to help and support me. They gave me financial and emotional support when it mattered the most. The act of checking in on me when I was silent, knowing that I likely wouldn't reach out, means more than I can ever say. They wanted me to know that they were still there, even in the silence. I prayed to God that I wasn't a burden to them.

I prayed that I would get stronger and that I would be able to survive this loss. That I would be able to have conversations again and perform at my new job, which I took to care for my family, even though I hated it.

He repeated, "Stop hiding and unmask yourself. Be present."

I was like, "Lord, I don't know how I can be present when I work two hours away and I'm driving four hours a day. I leave my house at five in the morning, and I get home at seven. How can I be present and do all the other things that you still need me to do, too?"

"Let it all go; let it all go," I heard in reply. I don't know what that means, but every time I sit with it and every time I pray, my house flashes, my car flashes, and my job flashes in front of me. All of it should be let go. If we don't take action, the universe will. I kept telling my husband, "I think we should just sell our house and move away, not buy another house. Like, not be tied down. Just sell our house, move away, homeschool our kids, and live a life of love and doing things that we want to do."

Every time I say that, it's almost as if I'm getting praise from the Lord. Every time I say that, fear is like, *Girl, what the hell is wrong with you? You know that's not ideal. You can't do that; quit your job, sell your house, and sell your cars. How are you gonna get anywhere? Where are your kids gonna live? How are you gonna feed them?*

But what I know right now is that they're living without a

mother, and that doesn't seem right either. So, instead of climbing the corporate ladder, I will be going a different way.

I've been numbing, shopping, and eating—doing all of these things, trying to comfort my pain. Trying to comfort the discomfort. Trying to make sense of why in the world God wants me to do this. What would happen if I sold my house and had no ties to a place where I felt so much trauma and shame? What if I quit my job and gave up those six figures? What if I took the leap of faith and went all in, with no burden besides taking care of my family and myself? What *would* happen then?

I can tell you what the vision brings. What I see is a hundred little masks shed. I see myself not living according to societal expectations, not trading my time for money, and not sacrificing my family. I see myself being present, being unmasked, being financially free, being physically, mentally, and emotionally *home*, and having joy in my life. Putting myself and the people that I love first is what I see when I follow that vision.

What I see when I follow the current roadmap I've been on is the life that I'm living now. And I have to ask myself: *Is it worth it?* No, it's not worth it.

Chapter 26

My Hero Didn't Wear A Cape

Shawn was not just my big brother; he was my hero. We went through so much together. He loved everyone so passionately and felt everything so deeply. Battling with insecurities and sadness, life just kept throwing him curveballs. We would often have conversations about when life would just give us a damn break. It never did come for Shawn, and I can't help but wonder, if it did, would life look drastically different? Would he still be alive?

I'll never know, but I have to believe he's in heaven with Jordan, Charlene, Papa, our stepdad Vinny, and so many more we've lost along the way. I'm going to share the letter I wrote to Shawn the day after he passed away and the same letter I read while standing at the head of his grave.

Dear Shawn (Shawny), you were my brother, my protector, and my best friend. The love and light you poured into the world were immense, and your loss has left an unfillable void in my heart. As my big brother, you stood in the line of fire, shielding me from harm and caring for me in ways that only a true protector could. You were the warrior against the world, shouldering burdens that many couldn't even fathom. You were more than just a brother to me; you were a hero, the best anyone could ever ask for. I look back now and wish for so many things. I wish I could have been a better little sister. I wish I could change certain things and make different choices. More than anything, I yearn for just one more moment with you. A moment to hold you close, to tell you how deeply proud I am of the person you were (every version of you), to express just how much I love you. But in my heart, I'm trying to find comfort, hoping that your pain and suffering are now over. Even though you are no longer physically with us, I believe you will continue to watch over us, protecting us just as you always did. You are an integral part of our forever, and your spirit continues to light our paths. In my heart, I carry our memories, our shared laughter, and our bond that nothing can break, not even death. I hold onto the knowledge that love is not confined by the mortal coil, and though you are no longer here in the flesh, you are forever a part of me. I miss you terribly, Shawny, but I know your spirit is at peace. I love you always and forever. Your little sister, Lexie

It's hard to find the right words to capture a lifetime of memories, laughter, and deep-rooted love. The world lost an extraordinary soul on July 26, 2023, but heaven gained a guardian angel. Shawn was my protector, my best friend, and the person who loved me more than anyone else.

I think back to our childhood, filled with the raw energy of wrestling matches as we walked out to WWE soundtracks, attempting to mimic the flair of the professionals. Or the game nights with just us and our mom, pizza boxes sprawled open and Big Slam sodas lining the table. He never let me win, but he always cheered the loudest when I finally did score a victory.

I remember our fishing adventures, where my makeshift stick and line somehow managed to catch more fish than Shawn's fancy gear. We'd laugh until our sides hurt, celebrating the simple joys of life. And who could forget our video gaming competition days? When our babysitter, Mary Lue, added her own hilarious sound effects while barely avoiding catastrophes with the controllers leaping out of her hands on several occasions, our poor TV suffered the impact. Ha, those were the days of living in joy and cherishing the little things.

As we grew older, we ventured into the world, living together in Virginia. That year was unforgettable for both of us. We had good and bad experiences, but he was always there for me, whether I needed a laugh or a shoulder to cry on. Even in those serious moments, Shawn's sense of humor never failed to come through. He was the cheerleader who believed in me, even when I didn't believe in myself. I was able to accomplish so many things because of his borrowed belief in me.

Shawn had this amazing gift of making everyone feel special. Whether it was giving away his last dollar or offering a random act of kindness to a stranger, his love and light touched countless lives. Now, every step without him feels heavier, but it's also a step that carries his memory. I hope he's looking down on us, free from any earthly struggles, his soul at peace. I miss him every single day, and that void will never be filled, but I find solace in the love and the memories that will forever be etched in my heart.

He was irreplaceable. And as his little sister, I pledge to honor his legacy by being as kind, loving, and selfless as he was.

Chapter 27

Unconditional Love

I struggled when Jordan died. His death amplified many worries and scary moments, wondering if something was going to happen to another child or if my husband would pull through. I worried about Jordan's mother, sister, brothers, grandparents, and aunts and uncles. I never truly understood what it meant to have a broken heart until I felt the physical, mental, and emotional pain of living through such an experience that shattered my world.

I know everyone says they have the best kids, but truly, we are blessed with our babies! Jordan and Corine were the two sweet kids who accepted me into their lives and loved me so deeply. What a privilege it was to get to love him.

Jordan and I really bonded when he was a teen. He got a job at my work and would stop in every afternoon to say hi and chat. I would conclude our routine by walking on the call room floor to give him a hug and tell him how much I loved him. Most kids would be repulsed by such an embarrassing act, but he never was. Even when kids would laugh and say, "I love you, too, Jordan." He was a kid who loved so deeply.

For most of my life, I asked God about love and what unconditional love would feel like, and he answered me by making me a mom—biological and bonus. Each of our kids is unique, and their superpowers are amazing.

Jordan's was his big love and ability to see everyone he encountered.

Corine's are her wittiness and ability to understand concepts beyond her years. Honestly, it's a true toss-up between her and her father, and Dan is literally one of the funniest people I know. And now, Corine is twenty. How did that happen so quickly? A wave of nostalgia washes over me, tinged with a bittersweet longing for those younger years. Yet, my heart also swells with pride as I consider the incredible young woman she's becoming. She still possesses that indomitable spirit, that unyielding will that so boldly announced itself on that recital stage years ago.

Ryan's superpowers are his empathy and creativity. His tenderness and ability to feel what others are feeling without them expressing it are incredible. And the art, games, and pure magic his mind creates keep me in awe of his talent. Such a special boy.

And Xander (Alexander) is so genuinely kind and ambitious. He is the kid who hurts when others hurt and wants to fix it. And his ambition, especially in sports, is incredible. He has this beautiful talent of not only learning things but also being able to memorize them, think on his toes, and see things most can't.

I think to myself every day, *How lucky am I to get to be their mother?* God could have taken away my ability to conceive, like the doctors told me was the case, but He decided I was worthy of getting such incredible examples of love. He has helped me see that as deeply as I want to love everyone else, I have to start with myself, and He's so kind that He let me borrow His vision and abundance of love. He gave me kids to admire, love, and cherish so I could find the little girl in me to love and cherish. And then one day, He decided to take one of those children I was privileged to love, and it crushed my heart so badly that the average person would never want to love again.

Today I sit here with a wounded heart, but an appreciation for the time I had with Jordan, the moments I got to love and guide him, and even more so for the moments he truly loved me.

October 3, 2022. That morning, the air itself seemed to sag with a weight I had never felt before. Everything turned into a blur, each moment carrying the unbearable weight of finality, of a future we had to face without Jordan.

Losing Jordan was one of the most devastating experiences of my life. A dark shadow fell upon all the joyful memories, casting a gloom that seemed almost sacrilegious to the radiant young man he was. The pressure was suffocating on my chest, and in that moment, I knew what true love was because I was experiencing unbearable heartbreak.

I can't describe the odd place a stepmother occupies in moments like these. The love I felt for Jordan was as real and as deep as any biological tie could forge, yet societal perceptions often diminished that connection. There were hushed voices and judgmental glances, veiled implications that because he was not "mine," my grief must be less significant and less valid. There were comments like, "You're doing it for attention," or

"You should be over it by now." These statements cut me to the core, deepening my sorrow with a sense of isolation.

They never understood. Jordan was one of the first children who loved me unconditionally. His love was pure, free from the complicated tensions that often arise in blended families. His heart, full of love for everyone he met, made him an extraordinary young man. He was the family clown, the master of board games, the kid who laughed heartily at his dad's jokes and filled the house with the most beautiful sounds, and the young man who appreciated whatever meal was put in front of him—even my culinary misadventures.

Jordan understood the essence of life in a way that eludes most adults. He valued time like the precious, fleeting commodity it is and chose to spend it on what really matters—family. He enriched all of our lives, filling our homes with warmth, laughter, and an endless reservoir of love.

No, Jordan was not my biological son, but in every way that counts, he was my child. And he always will be. My love for him defies titles, ignores bloodlines, and disdains societal expectations. It's a love that exists in the sacred spaces of my heart, untouchable by judgments and assumptions.

It's a love that's as eternal as the soul we so tragically lost. Even as I navigate this complex journey of grief, I find solace in the indelible impressions he left on my heart, my life, and on everyone who had the privilege to know him. And so, while October 3, 2022, marked the day we lost him, every other day marks the reality that we had him, that we loved him, that we were loved by him, and that we always will.

The memories of Jordan, as well as Corine's journey of growth, stand as my guiding lights—reminding me of the depth of love that we shared, the lives we touched, and the resilience of a blended family that faced the world, for better or for worse, together.

How I miss the sound of the front door swinging open and Jordan's voice ringing through the house: "Padre, where you at? I'm here; what's for dinner?" Those words, so simple yet so meaningful, are like echoes that still resonate in my heart and the walls of our home. How I'd give anything to hear them just one more time.

I also miss those weekends when Jordan and Dan would go shooting together, a father-son ritual that transcended the act itself and became a cherished tradition. They would come home loaded with "snacks," their code word for treasures acquired from their little adventures.

The moment Jordan stepped through the door and bellowed, "Snacks!" the other boys in the house would react as if summoned by a clarion call. It was like watching a herd of elephants trampling over each other, jockeying to get their hands on the choicest treats. In those simple, everyday moments, the essence of our family was captured—full of love, laughter, and a bit of playful chaos.

I find comfort in these memories, in the echoes of love and life that fill the void Jordan's departure has left in us. While these recollections are tinged with an unspeakable sorrow, they also hold within them a profound beauty. They serve as constant reminders that even though he's no longer physically with us, his spirit continues to touch every facet of our lives.

It's these seemingly trivial yet deeply meaningful instances that I hold onto and treasure the most. They remind me that love, in its purest form, isn't confined by societal norms or biological ties. It transcends all boundaries, filling our lives with warmth and making every moment worth living.

We talk about these stories as a family and with friends who never had the chance to meet Jordan. They offer valuable lessons in love, in the sheer power of family—whether blended or biological—and in the indomitable spirit of a young man who left us far too soon. And whenever I share these stories, the room is filled not just with my voice but also with Jordan's echoes—the laughter, the love, and the life that he brought into our world.

And so, he lives on—in the stories we share, in the memories we cherish, and in the love that refuses to dim even as the days, months, and years pass. Though the sorrow of losing him will never completely fade, these echoes of love offer glimpses of eternal joy, a reminder that his light will forever shine in our hearts.

Chapter 28

To My Inner Child

Dear Lexie,

LOVE. It should be such a simple word, simple to do, and uncomplicated to say, yet it remains the most complex word, feeling, choice, and investment there is. So beautifully broken, poetic, yet ugly. Love is ugly, love is raw, and love is freedom. We choose a simple word and create complexity around it.

Listen closely, Lexie. If I could bend time to talk to you at seven years old, this is what I would tell you. I see you staring at that Magic 8 ball, wondering if you're worthy of love. You live in a world where love feels transactional or even conditional. A kind smile for obedience. A quick hug for good behavior. I know how you tie your worth to these sporadic moments of "love" and how quickly they disappear with a misplaced expression or a poorly-timed question. I need you to know that what you're experiencing is not an accurate reflection of your worth or of love itself.

I'm thirty-six now, and what I've learned is that the love, or lack thereof, from others has everything to do with them and nothing to do with us. You are not a mirror reflecting other people's limitations; you are your own limitless universe. When I say limitless, I mean that the LOVE you're seeking is already within you. It's this cosmic, pulsing energy that fills your heart. It's not something anyone can give you or take away from you because you are its source. If I could envelop you in this wisdom right now, I would. Just remember, this is all temporary, and you will discover that LOVE is the energy YOU hold in your heart. This cannot be given or taken by anyone because the true source of LOVE is YOU.

Lexie, I know you don't fully understand what happened around you or why it happened to you. I look back at you with so much love and compassion, realizing that even when I was making choices—good or bad—all I was trying to do was protect us, to survive just a little longer, hoping something better would come along.

I wish I had realized sooner that the flicker of hope within us was so much more potent than the negativity trying to snuff it out. Many times, that flicker was just a small spark, but it was powerful. It kept us alive, moving forward even when it seemed like the whole universe was telling us to give up. That light was our own reservoir of unconditional love, a sacred gift from God. It's bigger than us, stronger than the darkness that tries to consume us. It's a war, yes, but not just for us but for many others, too.

This struggle isn't a solitary journey; it's part of a divine plan. It's the destiny God envisioned for us. You'll understand one day that the obstacles, the setbacks, the highs, and the lows are all pieces of a puzzle that only God knows how to solve. And the devil? He doesn't want us to complete it because he knows the impact we'll make when we do.

So hold on, little one. I promise our light is brighter than any darkness that tries to drown it out. And the love you're looking for? You already have it. It's been in you all along.

Listen to me, because there's so much I want to tell you about the journey ahead. From as early as you could feel, perhaps when you were just two, you felt an immense love welling up inside you. You sensed joy simply being around people; you yearned for the warmth of an embrace, and even then, you had this innate need to help, to heal, to be of service to others. You're a light waiting to ignite, yet, along the way, you'll find people and circumstances trying to snuff out your glow. Don't let them.

Oh, how you'll search for love! You'll seek it everywhere: in the foster home, from your mother, your father, and even from transient relationships that, alas, were designed more to hurt than to heal. You'll look for that special someone to sweep you off your feet, take away your pain, and help you forget all the world's cruelties. But listen closely: the one you've been seeking is already within you. The love you offer so freely to others is the love you must first extend to yourself.

There will be times when you'll silence your voice because you're afraid of sounding unintelligent. You'll measure your words by the yardstick of others' opinions, forgetting that what you have to say, what only you can express, is what's really needed. You are not here to echo; you are here to speak your own profound truth.

You see, God has given you an inexhaustible well of love and hope, one that you can draw from whenever the world makes you feel parched and dry. All the tribulations, all the setbacks, all the heartbreaks—they're God's way of breaking open new wells within you so that you can hold more love, more wisdom, and more resilience. So, trust in those moments when you feel closest to defeat; it's God showing you a different path, telling you that you're strong enough to traverse it.

In you is a roar that's yet to be fully unleashed. And once you remember how to use it and how to harness its power for change, courage, and compassion, the earth will quake, the heavens will sing, and hearts will awaken. Like King Arthur, only you have the strength to pull that sword from the stone. In your case, it's a different kind of might—the kind that transforms not just yourself but humanity.

You'll be tempted to lose yourself in others because you love them so deeply that it's almost unbearable. That love isn't a burden; it's your superpower. Don't mute it. Don't shy away from it. Embrace it, but remember to extend some of that embrace inward. You need your love as much as the world does. Don't serve others at the expense of yourself, or else the light that you're meant to shine will flicker and fade. It's not selfish to keep some of that incredible light for yourself; it's necessary.

There will come a time when you feel lost and unable to locate the constellation, and that's when your light will guide you home. Forget what's outside and focus on the galaxy within you. Let its light lead you back to your path.

You were never meant to be small, little one. Your light is meant to be blinding, your roar deafening, and your love all-encompassing. You are a force of nature, a tidal wave of compassion and strength. Never forget that. Hold onto this truth as tightly as you hold onto your dreams, and know that the brightest days are not behind you but ahead.

Xo,

Alexis

Chapter 29

Thank You God

Dear God,

Hey, G! It's me again. I just wanted to say a big, humongous "thank you" for showing me all I can be. It's like you've handed me this giant, colorful map and said, "Here's your adventure!" And, wow, what an adventure it's starting to look like.

Sometimes, I feel like I'm in a big, wild game of faith over fear. You're teaching me to leap through doors you fling open (even the ones that seem super scary at first) and to gently close the ones that aren't meant for me, no matter how much I want to peek inside. It's like you're whispering, "Trust me," and I'm learning to whisper back, "I do."

You're showing me my purpose, God, like a secret mission only I can do. And you're nudging me, ever so gently, to just let go and let you lead. I'm seeing the vision—the big picture you've painted—and all you're asking is for me to step into it. It's a bit like being given the lead role in the school play, and man, I want to make you proud.

But, oh boy, there are times when I hesitate, like when I'm standing at the edge of the high dive, looking down into the pool. Those moments of pause? They feel like forever. That's when I need your strength, G, to take the leap.

I feel your power in me, like I've got this superhero cape that only I can see. It makes me want to do amazing things—to spread kindness and light, just like you do. I want nothing more than to make you smile and to make you happy.

Yet, sometimes, when I'm feeling all pumped and ready, like I can conquer the world, that's when the challenges come knocking. The devil tries to crash my party, throwing everything he's got at me. And, yeah, sometimes I stumble and get a bit wobbly, but I remember your promise, dust myself off, and keep going. Because you've got my back, right, Lord? Even when I'm feeling like I'm in the last round, up against the ropes.

I've come a long way from my caterpillar days, munching leaves and wondering what's next. Then, there was my cocoon phase, all wrapped up, doing some serious soul-searching and healing. And now? Now I'm spreading my wings, ready to soar as the butterfly you always knew I could be. It's my time to shine, to show the world the beauty of my transformation, the power of faith, and the strength found in connection.

I'm not running from my destiny anymore, G. I'm running towards it, embracing and living it. So, please, keep believing in me, cheering me on, and guiding me. With you by my side, I can do anything. I'm ready for this journey, God, ready to be all I can be.

With all my heart (and butterfly flutters),

Your girl,

Lexie

Peace out.

Just kidding, amen.

Chapter 30

Final Words To The Reader

To My Sweet Friend,

As you turn the final page of *Changing The Reflection*, I wanted to extend a heartfelt thank you for joining me on this deeply personal journey. Sharing my story with you was not just an act of recounting memories; it was a profound declaration of living truthfully and courageously.

Each word in this book was written to challenge the silence that often shrouds our deepest struggles—the unspoken pains and the quiet battles we wage behind the smiles we wear. More than anything, I hope my story serves as a reminder that no matter the depth of darkness you face, there is an indomitable spirit within you capable of rising above it.

Now, I turn to you. Not just as a reader, but as a fellow human with dreams deferred and desires unspoken. Why wait? Why let another day pass without stepping into the fullness of your potential? The truth I've found on my journey, and one I hope you carry with you, is that waiting for the perfect moment often means missing the opportunity at hand. We are not promised tomorrow; we have only this moment to embrace our purpose and dive headfirst into our destinies.

Your circumstances, no matter how daunting, are temporary. They are merely obstacles meant to be overcome, not reasons to stand still. In your hands, you hold not just a book but a call to action—a call to say yes to yourself, to your dreams, and to the life you deserve to live.

So, I urge you not to see it as an end but as a beginning. A starting point from which you can leap towards your dreams with courage, knowing that the strength to overcome and thrive resides within YOU.

Say yes to your life. Say yes to your dreams. Say yes to being the architect of your destiny. The time is now, and it's yours to seize.

With all my love and encouragement,

Alexis Carpenter

Acknowledgments

This book is not just a product of my efforts but the culmination of countless hours of support, encouragement, and inspiration from a circle of extraordinary people to whom I owe immense gratitude.

First and foremost, I owe an immeasurable debt of gratitude to my family. To my husband, Dan Carpenter, whose love and support are my foundation, and to my children, Jordan, Corine, Ryan, and Xander, who have generously shared their time and hearts, allowing me the space to create. Your sacrifice and selflessness have made all of this possible.

I am deeply thankful to my mother Penny, sister Adrienne, brothers Shawn and Jason, aunts, uncles, and grandparents. Your collective presence in my life has been a constant source of strength and joy. Each of you has contributed to this journey in ways that words cannot fully capture.

A heartfelt thank you to Burning Soul Press, especially Lauren Eckhardt, Allison, and Karen, for believing in my vision and nurturing it to fruition. To my Soulful Author Journey family —Debbie, Krystee, and many others—your camaraderie and shared passion have been a ray of sunshine.

Special thanks go to my mentors and friends, Jen Gottlieb and Chris Winfield, whose guidance has been pivotal. Lindsey Schwartz and Hannah Wells, thank you for your roles in my personal and professional growth. To the Girl Gang community, your vibrant spirit and collective strength have been a constant source of motivation.

To my beautiful friends, Darcey Elizabeth and Jamie Sink, thank you for the friendship and love that have nourished my soul through this intense period of creation. Your support has not only lifted me but has also been a fundamental part of this journey.

Each of you has touched this project and my life in invaluable ways. I am eternally grateful for your contributions, big and small, seen and unseen. Thank you for being part of this incredible journey.

About the Author

Alexis Carpenter was born in Troy, New York, in 1987 and moved to Vermont at the age of six, where she has spent most of her life, scattered with travels that have added a dash of adventure to her experiences.

Throughout her journey with writing, Alexis has collaborated on articles for Authority Magazine, CanvasRebel, and Claim Your Worth Magazine. She also curates insightful content for her two LinkedIn newsletters, Her Executive Closet, and The Weekly Collective, where she shares her expertise and engages with a diverse audience.

To discover more about Alexis and follow her literary and life adventures, connect with her on social media and visit her website:

Instagram:@alexismcarpenter
Facebook:Alexis Carpenter
LinkedIn:Alexis M Carpenter
raisinghopellc.org

Finding My Voice

In the quiet moments, I find my truth,
A whisper soft, yet strong as youth.
Through pain and loss, my heart does mend,
A journey of self-love without end.

I seek my voice, once lost, now found,
In every beat, a sacred sound.
No longer bound by others' will,
I stand alone, my spirit still.

With every breath, I claim my space,
A testament to my own grace.
For in my heart, a fire does burn,
A love for self, a voice I've earned.

Xx,
Alexis

Scan the QR Code to be taken to all the exclusive supplemental material:

www.ingramcontent.com/pod-product-compliance
Lightning Source LLC
Chambersburg PA
CBHW030519080526
44586CB00011B/248